Magnolia

The Benefits of Adversity

BHAKTI MARY

ISBN: 978-0-9968246-1-3

Editorial credit to Michael Beloved, Marcia Beloved and Mark Wills.

Cover design by Michael Beloved.

Email: brownBerryBooks@gmail.com

Website: www.brownBerryBooks.com

Now and then,
it is good to pause
in our pursuit
of happiness
and just be happy.

Guillaume Apollinaire

MAGNOLIA

Contents

MAGNOLIA

5

MAGNOLIA

Introduction

One thing that you can be certain of is that your experience is not unique to you. Somewhere in the world, there is another human going through the same things if not worse things. Keep life and experiences in that perspective and stay on your feet.

No matter how hard things get, they can also turn quickly to something wonderful. Ground to something so that you can understand the volatility and stability that life provides. Be ready for both.

The hardest part about life is heartbreak and the most wonderful part of life is love itself. Love yourself so you always have something to come back to...you can always return home.

Dedication

This book is dedicated to my children, Alessandro, Nora and Liam. I hope you will find some wisdom in my words. You make my heart overflow with joy.

Special recognition to my parents, Michael and Marcia, and brother Dear who encouraged me to write and publish.

Love to my husband, Mark for believing in me and encouraging me. I appreciate you immensely.

A big hug to Draupadi, Misty, Charlynda, Nicole, Monique, and Bloom whose support and love in all circumstances have made me a better person.

Thank you to every person who gave me the courage to be vulnerable and to take one more step towards finding and revealing my authentic self. Open vulnerability assessments often lead to hypocritical judgment. I hope you will read my book without judgment.

PART 1

Thoughts and Speech

So many thoughts, ideas, and memories stay locked inside our heads. No one sees them but they drive and guide our behaviors and choices. Many of us have fabricated a world inside of our heads full of lies and assumptions or fantasies. Inside we have layered all our experiences, most of which only we are familiar with and we expect that others will understand the framework and foundation from which we operate. But, no one can fully assume our position or stand on our foundation and so we must work internally to operate from somewhere that is positive and beneficial to those we interact with. What can we do to improve the quality of what is swimming around in our consciousness?

I have always had optimistic thoughts despite some heart wrenching life experiences. Thoughts often translate to expression and speech. My friends always say that if looks could kill, I would be a serial killer, and it is a good thing that I am not often as upset as I look. I remember the painful gut check when my fiancé told me that he "hated the way I looked" at him at times. I think he wished that I would look at him with contentment and joy and I understand why. There is a vulnerability associated with me smiling and showing other outward indicators of contentment and joy. I do not feel that I was raised to feel joy and, in my most vulnerable relationship, I still feel uncomfortable expressing it freely in expression and speech.

With that said, the words we say matter! Listening to ourselves can reveal areas to improve upon. If you are bad at listening to yourself, just ask the people around you. Feedback is a wonderful thing when we use it constructively to improve. I guarantee if your spoken and unspoken words are harmful, someone around you has noticed!

1

Definition of Self

Who are you? On a "Hello. I am _____" nametag, we might write our name, but if someone asked you to describe who you are, how would you answer? This is one of the most profound questions you can ask yourself. The term "self" describes your identity. How would you like to permanently experience your true self? Your answer probably depends on your definition of self. What is your true identity? Discovering the answer to this question requires honest thought about who you are in the open and behind closed doors. Are you prepared to be honest with yourself?

DEFINING YOUR SELF

Do you lead a double life or does the real you permeate in all aspects of your life? Caitlyn Jenner lived as a male for 65 years, but it was so far from who she really was. Are you a different person at work, at home, and with your friends? Are you friendly to everyone at work but then go home to verbally abuse your children or significant other?

Many of us feel like our work defines us on the job but at home we lack the control we have at work or the recognition we may achieve at work. The truth is that if you are not in control, you must at least know who you are so you can operate out of kindness to others. When we lack internal self-definition, this can manifest in a desire to look outside of ourselves for definition.

We are the only ones who will be judged by our actions, not the others whom we based our self on.

— Paul Sposite —

Do you let others define you? After I got divorced in 2009, my next boyfriend said that every time I spoke Spanish, he was reminded that I was some other guy's wife and he was just there for what was left. I had come up for a written nickname of him "miGuAn" which stood for "My Guardian Angel". The words "Mi" reminded him of my ex-husband who spoke Spanish. Instead of thinking of how I positively had identified him as a guardian angel to me, he chose to use it to frame me negatively. Somehow, what was left of me in his mind was less than what was there before.

What was left? Me. So many people in my life have tried to tell me that I was not worth much. While I have made many mistakes and sometimes done things that I am not proud of, that does not make me worthless. If you are fortunate, you are surrounded by people who do not make you feel this way but much of the world wants to make others feel like they are less in order to prop themselves up. Some of us even put others on a pedestal as an excuse to invoke self-pity upon ourselves and our perceived lower position. All of this began to matter less when I finally learned that self-definition had to come from within. No matter how much more or less I possessed than others, their definition of their self and my definition of myself became clear only when we individually looked inside.

People often define themselves externally by their looks, associations, material possessions and professions. Who we know and associate with can also be a quick and convenient way of defining ourselves. Others may define us by our shortcomings or our accomplishments. By defining ourselves in this manner, we restrict our own ability to feel self-worth. We rely on looking right, performing right, having the right car, having the right job, our relationships with important people, someone's approval of us, or knowing the right people for our self-worth. We may begin to believe that something is wrong, defective, flawed, unimportant, unworthy, or inadequate with ourselves. Things do not define you. People do not define you. Jobs do not define you. The truth is, nothing outside of you can define you. You define you. All power to define you is in self.

When we perform honest self-examination to learn about who we really are, we move beyond external definitions into internal definitions.

REDEFINING SELF

Think for a moment about what you really value in others. You might find that you value traits such as honesty, kindness, generosity, compassion, understanding, empathy, and acceptance. Now, accept the responsibility for defining yourself. Take a moment to write down and start to define yourself in positive ways. Then, ensure your actions consistently align with your positive definition. For some of us, we may need to change the way we behave. The good news is that it is never too late for a realignment.

TAKING ACTION FOR PERMANENT EXPERIENCES OF SELF

Action follows definition – your definition affects the decisions you make and actions you take. By acting on your self-definition, you create lasting positive habits that will form the authentic you. Consistent actions across all areas of your life determine who you are. Your actions reflect your thoughts – a reflection of your inner self. Every action is a result of a thought.

> *The most powerful relationship you will*
> *ever have is the relationship with*
> *yourself. It is in this relationship that you*
> *set the standard for all others.*
>
> — Steve Maraboli —

How do you want people to define you? Does it matter how others define you? If your actions are consistent in all areas of your life, people will respect you – the true and authentic you. They will understand that the outside of you matches the inside of you. Be brave! Abandon the multiple and often conflicting sides of yourself if you have them. Create your new ideal – be yourself and solidify your authentic self with congruent actions in all areas of your life.

2

Evolve Your Definition of Self

Realize and internalize that the definition of self never stops. Defining ourselves is a lifelong dynamic process. The more we know, the better we do and the more we can evolve. As we progress through life in various levels of physical, mental, emotional and spiritual development, our sense of self will continue to refine and mature. In this refinement and maturation, it does not help to beat ourselves up through excessive self-criticism. By allowing change to freely evolve, one may gently and gradually awaken to authenticity. Let us look at how people can develop a sense of fulfillment and competency in the physical, mental, emotional, and spiritual realms.

PHYSICAL: Here, a person derives their sense of fulfillment and competency from physical achievements (i.e. sports, violence, benevolent service) but quickly realizes that someone who is stronger or even an injury can take away this sense of fulfillment leaving one feeling weak. In college and even after, I noticed that many athletes exist in this realm. Their self was largely defined by the sport they played. After they played the last game or suffered significant loss in their sport, it took some time to find their center again.

MENTAL: Here, a person derives their sense of fulfillment and competency from successful use of their brain power but realizes over time that mental capacity can fade and comparison to smarter people can take away this sense of fulfillment leaving one feeling inadequate. We see this mental existence clearly when someone of great academic success suddenly loses their ability to feel accomplished. This could occur at retirement, job loss, illness, or even if someone smarter comes along. In the mental framework, one's success may largely be defined by the job or position they hold or the discoveries they have made in an academic realm.

EMOTIONAL: Here, a person derives their sense of fulfillment and competency from the love and emotional support of others, but this too can be taken away at a moment's notice. During a breakup or in loss, we can see how much someone is defined by the emotional support of another human being. It is the prolonged reliance upon this that can be limiting. When someone is in an abusive relationship but has difficulty leaving, we often find that they are not sure who they would be outside of that relationship. Yet inside the relationship, they are sad and bound.

SPIRITUAL: Here, a person recognizes that personal fulfillment is realized through freedom from the world. This is sometimes referred to as enlightenment.

The true self requires no rationalization or justification. When our daily experiences reflect the natural attributes of our authentic and true self, we are free.

Many people associate spirituality with a religion but when you can exist through experiences that demonstrate your authentic and true self, I believe you are living a spiritually charged life. This kind of life transcends age and accomplishment. When you live a spiritual life, you live freely.

Love Thyself First

We have all heard the quote love thyself. Most of us probably know someone who is really into themselves and we may have even negatively labeled them as a narcissist. I have noticed that these people are generally not well liked by people around them. They may be viewed as self-centered, arrogant or stuck up. Upon closer examination, this viewpoint tends to originate from someone who lacks self-love. People who lack self-love often envy those who love themselves and find it difficult to love others. They also want others to feel obligated to do things for them that are pleasing to them in order to create temporary bursts of love which cannot be sustained in the long term. People who do not love themselves are exhausting to be around.

Negative thought patterns infiltrate and corrupt our ability to stand on the solid foundation that self-love provides. Positive thoughts are essential to loving yourself.

Years ago, a boyfriend thought I was becoming too attached to him for the wrong reasons, and he offered some helpful advice which I have never forgotten. He said "Imagine that you are going to an important event. You are dressed in an exquisite dress and you are beautiful. You love the dress you have on. That is -- you as a single person. Now imagine that I am an accessory such as a bracelet, pair of earrings, ring, hairpiece, etc. You are prepared to go to the party with no accessories and you love the way you look in the exquisite dress. Now choose me, your accessory. We look great together, but we also look great alone." He was emphasizing that I conducted myself in a manner indicating that I was not whole without him. I can now admit that I was using him to become whole, and thus, our relationship was doomed to fail.

He recognized that I did not feel whole without him. If you are whole without others, then others can freely accompany you in life to accentuate and complement the person you already are. If you hate the dress you are wearing to a party, there is no accessory that can make you love the dress. I have never forgotten this lesson! Since then, I have worked diligently to love myself. Believe it or not, you must love yourself first. Anyone, including significant others/ spouses, dates, parents, friends or teachers, who lead you to believe otherwise, is misleading you.

- ✓ Know that mistakes are helpful. Each setback is an opportunity to improve. Mistakes are the lessons that prepare us to optimize our potential.

- ✓ Make peace with your past and any painful memories.

- ✓ Learn to enjoy the present and make healthy decisions today regardless of what happened yesterday.

Love presents itself on this journey called life. When you have reached a point in life where you can love self, you have awoken. How good is that? AWAKEN and be present! Love self! Recognize and accept your uniqueness. Believe in the masterpiece you are. Stop the self-criticism and negative thought patterns. Realize the satisfaction of being confident and use this to propel you into positively contributing to your environment. The world will tell you differently!

On a flight, I saw an ad run by Selective Search where apparently executive search meets personal matchmaking. The idea is Selective Search can find the perfect match for highly discriminating men and women. Think about it...you are one of billions of people surrounded by people trying to weed you out and find reasons why you are not the perfect match. And when you are matched with someone, sometimes they spend your entire time together trying to mold you into what they think is their perfect match – not just their accessory but their foundation for self-love – a void that no one person can exclusively fill.

Loving self is paramount.

You might be thinking, and rightly so, that there is more to the love thyself quote. Love thyself AND thy neighbor. I believe that those who are still learning to love themselves often struggle to love others.

Recognizing and accepting ourselves as we are is taking notice that we are not carbon copies of anything. We are each beautifully unique in our own regard. Love who you are and love who others are. Just be! Accept others and allow them to just BE too — just do not be invasive or allow others to invade your space.

4

Self Love Is The Starting Point

When reading *Nothing Changes Until You Do* by Mike Robbins, something I read struck me! In Chapter 9 titled Love Yourself (And the Rest Will Follow), Mike discusses the importance of self-love as the foundation and starting point for conscious growth and development. Self-love is the starting point!

The most important and final relationship we will ever be in is the relationship with self. Love is unconditional and when we have conditional self-love, Mike says it is just approval, not love.

I began to ponder on some routine conversations I have with several people very close to me. I also began thinking about whether I operated from a place of self-love. I know a few people that just cannot seem to celebrate themselves when things are not going well. They convey a state of sorrow and negativity to everyone that approaches them. Frequently, they want me to engage in a pity party with them because they do not approve of themselves on a day or in a moment. Some of these people do not remain my friend for long. The reason is that if I were to tell you 100 times how amazing you are and you tell me 100 times how terrible you are, we could be in that vicious cycle forever.

Friends do not exist to prop one another up 100% of the time! However, it is more difficult when this person is a sibling, parent, or significant other. How can we encourage self-love amongst our inner circle?

The first step is to understand the importance of self-love. Quite often, I would be doing something silly around the house and my ex-boyfriend would say to me, "You just love yourself do not you?" to which I would respond with a smile, "Yes I do!" It sounds like I am full of myself, but I remind myself and you that self-love is healthy love. I was not always that way.

There were many days (and now only some days) that I went to sleep in tears because I believed that I was not good enough. There were many days when I felt rejected by others and lacked a foundation from which to believe that I was always enough.

There were many days when I dwelled on what people thought of me. We can learn to reduce our dwelling periods and to respond to the ebbs and flows of emotional sabotage generated by self or others better.

Self-love is the pulse of the soul and the health of the inner heart. Without it, we are unhappy weak spirits. We are doormats, and we are houses without doors.

That same boyfriend went on to become an ex fiancé and months after we broke up, he texted me to say, "You have ruined me for dating or getting married. You are one in a billion. There are no single women like you. Men leave their wives for women like you. They will obviously risk their careers for women like you. Women do not have the combination of beauty, personality, brilliance, career, and humor you have. It is pointless."

Some people like someone who is crazy about them, but for me, it was not enough. What about him? What did he think of himself? He lacked self-love and definition at that time which is why our relationship stood no chance of surviving. When I would ask him what he liked about himself, he came up empty handed every time – literally, every time. If someone is nothing without you, then they are also nothing with you. Of course, what he said was not entirely true – less than a year later, he got married.

By the way, for those relationships that simply have not worked for us, we must just LET THEM GO. Learn your lessons, walk away, and do better in the next one. We often judge one another for our relationships but relationships are the hardest thing we maneuver through and the focus should be on improvement; if we find that we cannot improve, then we should stop participating in the relationship saga where there is an expectation, and rightfully so, of positive interaction.

What impacts self-love? Our thought patterns are the single greatest factor of self-love. Self-love is an energy within that is manifested when we LIVE. I have always challenged people to "own their energy". Not sure what your energy is? Look at the people around you; they are a mirror. If you do not operate from a place of love, do not expect to attract it or for it to stick around. Positive people will flee from our presence because they cannot exist in any sustained manner around someone who is not operating from love. It is important to study and recognize negative thought patterns within ourselves because they are particularly disruptive!

Negative thought patterns drive you to 1) be obsessed with perfection, 2) believe nothing is ever good enough, 3) find something wrong with nearly every situation, 4) compare yourself to others in a manner that results in you believing you are not good enough and 5) constantly live your life based on what you think others will think, love and accept. The recognition and awareness of such thought patterns can be life-changing. If you are not sure, ask a few people who are close to you. If you have these thoughts, chances are you are operating with them as a foundation and the people around you have noticed. It will take significant effort on your part to get rid of the negative thought patterns.

If you do not approve of yourself, where can you go? What can you achieve?

I challenge you to love yourself.

5

Are You Talking To Yourself?

In 2014, I was washing breakfast dishes in our work break area, and my director Cara walked in the door. I smiled at her and said, "Good morning". She immediately began laughing and said, "You caught me talking to myself." I replied, "I had not noticed. Sometimes the best person to talk to is yourself." She replied, "I guess you're right." We will not always have someone next to us to engage in positive dialogue with and no matter how dark life becomes, we must be able to return to a positive thought. The ability to do so with predictability and speed is required for self-preservation and survival.

Do not be afraid to talk to yourself. Do not be afraid to consciously hold conversations with yourself and with friends. Most importantly, make sure these conversations are honest. For us to be blatantly honest with friends, we must trust that we can work through areas of confusion, vulnerability, and weakness with them. Notice I used the word work implying that we make progress and utilize the friendship as a sounding area not a dragging area. No true friend wants to be drug down with you into the depths of unhappiness or depression on a regular basis.

In my life, I realize that certain beliefs or concepts that guide me are not conventional and perhaps in order to be in a position to change these, I require honest real dialogue with people I can trust to uncover the driving factors and emotional gaps behind my behavior.

What happens with self-talk is you stimulate your action, direct your action and evaluate your action.

— Antonis Hatzigeorgiadis —

I frequently hold conversations with myself about focusing on the present. I have found it to be an effective practice to help me change troublesome behavior patterns. Talking to yourself in a respectful manner is a healthy practice particularly if it propels you into becoming your best self.

You do not have to wait for years to make your life better. You can do it today using positive self-talk. What you say when you talk to yourself changes

who you are right now, and it
guarantees your future will be different
from your past. Not only will it be
different, it will be better if you put
positive things into your mind.

— Dr. David Abbott —

I offer three personal examples of how I use self-talk to improve my focus on listening and the present.

Example 1: Someone will come up to my desk at work and want to hold a conversation with me. Secretly, I want to continue typing on my computer or I want to check my email. I can type without looking at the keyboard, and I used to do this when people were talking to me. After years of reflection, I have realized that if something is important, it requires my full attention. When people are talking to me, I cannot listen if I am busy with ten other things. Therefore, I tell myself, "Continue actively listening. This person and their words are important. Whatever you were working on can wait."

Example 2: I will be having a conversation with my son. I want to continue with whatever household chore I was doing while he continues talking to me.

This way I can accomplish two things at once! My son does appreciate and need my full attention at times. Therefore, I tell myself, "Remain focused on what he is saying. He is important to you as you are important to him. Whatever you were doing does not need to be completed immediately. You will have plenty of time for it later."

Example 3: In a heated conversation with my significant other, I want to get angry. Just the listening aspect can diffuse some of our disagreements. If I listen, I may find that we agree or that there is nothing to gain from continuing the argument. Therefore, I tell myself, "Becoming unglued is not the answer. Allow him to fully express himself. Remember your tone and volume. Continue listening. Try to see his points."

My self-talk often directs my actions. It serves as my internal compass and is an active reminder of the direction I would like to take in a situation. Does it always work? No, but I would say that 80-90% of the time, I am able to exhibit a positive behavior because of my internal dialogue.

I often watch loved ones lash out in a burst of anger when they feel upset. And the speed at which they do so without even realizing it means it is a programmed response to a feeling. The problem with this is that it is without regard to that person and how they should be treated. No internal dialogue has filtered the anger. The internal dialogue tends to happen after the damage has been done and saying sorry repeatedly for programmed destructive behavior tends to ring hollow on the receiver's ears because it is a reactive not proactive approach. The people we interact with deserve a proactive approach to behavior directed at them.

Practicing positive self-talk to reform behaviors can be effective.

6

Listening To Yourself Speak

Have you ever listened to the words you speak? This is what Linus Mundy suggests as Idea #20 in the book Slow-down Therapy for rediscovering time and life. It made me think — so many times I have been advised to listen to others when they speak. But there is probably equal benefit to listening to the words I say.

Listening goes farther than hearing the words you speak. It also involves a self-examination with the goal of truly understanding ourselves.

In the book Seven Thousand Ways to Listen: Staying Close to What is Sacred, Mark Nepo defines listening as "the doorway to everything that matters. It enlivens the heart the way breathing enlivens the lungs. We listen to awaken the heart...to stay vital and alive." The act of listening is difficult due to all the external and internal distractions but an active effort to listen to both ourselves and others can be a game changer.

Try talking less today. Listen to your words and consider whether you really need to say what you are saying. You do not like listening to BS, so be part of the solution and stop uttering it.

Talk at the appropriate tone and level. Instead of raising your voice to speak to others, go to them and then speak at a reasonable level. No one else needs to hear the conversation. Remember your tone and/or volume is what usually makes people tune you out.

Speak unto others as you would have them speak onto you. As you speak, think – would I like to be spoken to this way? While this can be hard when you are in a heated or engaged discussion, take time to think after if you embodied the Golden Rule.

Audrey McLaughlin says "When you listen, it's amazing what you can learn. When you can act on what you've learned, it's amazing what you can change." And don't we all wish to be the change? There is always another conversation coming up during which we can listen to ourselves and learn ways to be better.

7

Avoiding Yourself

Most people go through each day in consistent and complete distraction because it is the easy way to live. Being distracted means you never stop and focus on yourself. To think about who you are is often hard and uncomfortable. This results in not being able to let go of people, experiences, and possessions because that is what we have become and we either are afraid of what will be left without these things or we are afraid to face them altogether.

Without these things, we feel alone and afraid. Fear sets in. We cannot listen to our own thoughts even for five minutes. We must pick up the phone. We must turn away from the show that makes us think about struggle and hardship. We must find the bar. We must watch the sports game. We must eat the food. We must work late. We must avoid ourselves by any means necessary.

I personally have learned to enjoy the isolation because I am introverted, and I like myself. At the same time, I struggle to be present with people, possessions and experiences. This is not necessarily a bad thing if these people, possessions and experiences are around you but preventing you from living your best life. The key is to be selective. I know my truth – I know what I am uncomfortable with about myself but now I protect myself from others.

What am I protecting myself from? Sometimes I think that if you are not even vulnerable with yourself, then we should not be vulnerable together. It is during the times when you are vulnerable and honest with yourself that you learn how to be compassionate to others in their moments of vulnerability with you.

8

You Are More Than A Number!

I have a lot of friends who are focused on their weight for better or for worse. I have tried for a long time to listen to and understand their struggles. In 1999, I applied for entry into the Air Force Academy. I went to the Military Entrance Processing Station (MEPS) which is a Department of Defense organization charged with determining an applicant's physical qualifications, aptitude and moral standards as set by each branch of military service, the Department of Defense, and federal law.

At the time, the minimum weight standard for a female at 66 inches height was 108 pounds. I was a mere 99 pounds. I decided that I would put on a lot of extra clothes for the weigh-in. I put on several jackets and extra layers of pants. When I was ready to step on the scale, the person weighing me asked me if I would like to remove my jacket and I said no. I was at a MEPS facility in Mississippi, and there was absolutely no reason for me to have that many clothes on.

Luckily for me, I had added enough weight, and I was offered entry into the United States Air Force Academy Preparatory School. Since that entry in 1999, I have gained 30 pounds in 19 years. I still get accused of looking thin and having "no meat on my bones".

While I do not exercise a lot, I do try to eat healthy. I do not measure calories each day. I have indulgent eating days and disciplined eating days. I love to eat, and I also love a good discussion on healthy eating habits. I am self-conscious about my weight too.

Even though some people think I look too thin, there are people close to me who notice and comment on the fact that I have gained weight. The most annoying and memorable comments came from a boyfriend who used to comment when I gained a few pounds due to bloating. This boyfriend even said that if I were to want to become pregnant, perhaps I should get in better shape first. Unfortunately, no perfect state exists, not for me and not for you.

I do not understand fully the struggle that comes with being overweight and the struggle to curb unhealthy eating habits or the struggle to learn to enjoy exercise. While I can empathize with the struggle, I also know that a deliberate lack of self-control and prolonged emotional emptiness often leads to the practice of unhealthy eating habits – a state in which we lack self-love.

What I know for sure is that you are more than a number. You are more than the pounds on the scale. You are more than the calories consumed each day or the measure on your Fit Bit. You are more than the number of steps you took today. You are more than your age. You are more than the number of miles you run. You are more than the weight you lift. You are more than the minutes you exercise. You are more than the number of diets you have tried and retried.

You are more than a number. Stop focusing on the number. Escape the number. Figure out who you are first and foremost. Reflect on yourself. Discover what makes you happy. Then, align your exercise and weight goals accordingly.

I think as a society we are in a vicious cycle. We think if we are an optimal weight, then we will be happy. When we cannot reach this optimal weight, we are not happy. For some, setting a goal to reach a target weight results in a state of depression.

Perhaps the number of pounds you weigh is not the source of your happiness and never will be. Remember there is no such thing as perfection but there is progression. People who tell you otherwise are simply unrealistic, unreasonable, and out of touch with reality.

Maybe if we are happy, we will be better positioned to reach our health goals (not, I will be happy when I reach my health goal). What if you concentrate on being happy right now? Life's problems or happiness are not fixed or achieved by eating or dieting. Next, you must truly believe that you can achieve certain results or that you can exercise a certain degree of self-discipline and control. As people progress towards a certain weight, they also become used to seeing that weight in the mirror. The weight becomes a physical mask and barrier to emotional shortfalls and rather than do the work, most accept the status quo – they take refuge in the barrier they have created. If you are reading this and some of it rings true, consider a new approach to your journey of weight loss.

9

Value Who You Are, Not What You Do

Do you know someone who defines themselves by what they do? Does their career or personal accomplishments or failures make them happy or sad? Do you know someone who wallows in sorrow at the first sign of difficulty, challenge, or hurdle? If they cannot succeed at work, do they take it out on their spouses or friends or children when they come home? Are you that person? Am I that person?

At a marriage conference I attended called Life to Remember, the audience was encouraged to do something very important – Value Who You Are, Not What You Do. We cannot anticipate the certainty of difficulties and problems nor can we always respond properly to them or guarantee control of the results from our actions.

I have numerous Post-It Notes at work filled with short three-word reminders that keep me grounded. One reminder says "let go of results".

This means to begin each day as I am. Socrates said, "Man, know thyself." I assess myself. I perform work throughout the day based on who I am – doing the best that I can. I work from my soul – the center of my being – the inner me. After that, regardless of what happens, I try to let go of the results.

It is not easy to let go of results each time and I must treat each day as a learning laboratory. The results do not dictate happiness or sadness – the person I am dictates whether I choose happiness or sadness as a response to events. Has anyone ever told you after a negative event – "Do not beat yourself up?" They are saying let go of results – you are not your results but you must learn from them. I encourage you to begin to use your responses to results to draw you closer to your true self.

Show who you are. Be defined by who you are. Be remembered for the type of person you were – not the job you did.

At any funeral I have ever attended, the message is usually either about "who someone was" or "what someone did". If the message was primarily about "what someone did", it is because no one remembered or knew "who they were".

Maintain emotional consistency by developing a sound inner foundation. View challenges, successes and failures as opportunities to build on, refine, or develop your inner self. Start to value who you are.

Ask yourself the following important questions:

- ✓ What is important to me?

- ✓ How do I respond to failure?

- ✓ How do I respond to success?

- ✓ Does my job define me?

- ✓ How do people describe me?

- ✓ How would I describe myself?

- ✓ Do I strongly identify with successes and failures?

Also, take time to reflect on specific life experiences which challenge you or prevent you from knowing who you are. Become self-scheming to overcome these.

10

Be A Possibility Model

In 2008, Lance DeViney said to me "Bhakti...well, despite how things might have been going, you often had a great smile and were a breath of fresh air."

It is amazing how quickly the compliments of others can fade away. Life starts to happen and someone comes into life and chases away the memories that should sustain us forever. It is true. There are so many people whose memories have lasted with me and this was not one until I looked back at some early Facebook posts. One good thing social media can do for us is create a time capsule of memories - good and bad of what others said to us and what we said to others.

It has been over 15 years since I have seen or talked to Lance DeViney, an experienced and respected engineer in my professional career field. Looking back on his simple words made me smile. During a period of my life when I was stationed overseas for the first time, newly married, extremely far from home, a new mother, learning a new job, achieving a master's degree amongst other new and strange things, I learned many hard lessons and I still managed to thrive. I always believed in the possibility of today and tomorrow.

This same spirit has carried me through some tough times - some self-imposed and others simply endured. It is the idea that we keep trying no matter what. Regardless of what is going on or what has happened or what is about to happen, find a way to always learn and be excellent. Find a way to survive and to live and thrive in another moment. Never give up!

11

Facing Your Layers of Self-Doubt

Everyone faces self-doubt in varying degrees. Most people have been accumulating layers of self-doubt for decades. Imagine going to the North Pole. You are outside in extremely cold temperatures, and you have dressed to stay warm which means you have layer upon layer of clothing from head to toe.

Now imagine that you wear these same clothes when you sit on a St. Lucia beach. People with layers of self-doubt tend to never shed a layer no matter what circumstance they are in. Their voice-over is "I am not good enough", "I cannot do this", "I am not smart enough", "I have never done it this way", "I am not pretty enough" and so on. These voices speak authoritatively throughout each day and prevent people from "doing the work" as they face a variety of what appear to be daunting circumstances. Negative thought patterns can be difficult to purge.

When you are on that St. Lucia beach with those North Pole layers, no one can see the real you – as you hide in what you perceive to be a safe place. The truth is - that 'safe place' is downright miserable. You are uncomfortable and afraid inside. That 'safe place' is a place where your potential stays buried, your true emotions remain hidden, your friends and family remain distant, and your actions are determined by your fears. You act out of fear and lack of confidence.

Self-doubt is the fuel of fear — a fear of self! And self-doubt resides in your mind — in your thoughts. When you doubt self, you allow fear to dominate you. You dramatize situations repeatedly and try to recruit others to validate your fears so you can feel justified in the fear-dominated decisions you are making in your life. You know that you are paralyzed and are infinitely far from realizing your purpose and fulfilling your potential because the obstacles in front of you seem like they might as well be permanent. You believe this because change seems too risky. You are always uncertain and hesitant inside. Over time, you surround yourself only with people like yourself. Self-doubt escalates to the point that you make decisions based on what others project on you and not what you want for yourself. By doing this habitually, second-guessing yourself and the "self-pity" debilitates you.

By fully experiencing and going beyond an emotional block– through the layers of doubt and fear–you experience the emotion of who you truly are.

— Stephen Richards —

Let me offer a new approach. In this five-step approach, you are in control and you are responsible for yourself.

1. <u>Begin a gratitude journal</u>. For 30 days, decide to be consciously grateful and document this throughout your day (through words, photos, receipts, etc.) as you feel positive emotions. Stop drowning in self-pity by focusing on what you lack. CHOOSE to focus on what you ARE accomplishing and what DO have. Foster the feeling of gratitude. Describe why you are grateful for people and things. Write slowly, feeling and savoring each word. As you grow this habit, expand your awareness and really experience the world you are living in. Most importantly, keep it positive. You can

print shorter statements of gratitude to carry with you to reference in moments when the layers of self-doubt reassert themselves. Continue your gratitude journal as you progress through the next steps.

2. <u>Document the areas of self-doubt and associated emotions</u>. After you have developed the habit of identifying areas of gratitude, you are ready to start some of the hard work. Take one week to write down areas of your life where you notice that qualities like hatred, bitterness, envy, jealousy, resentment, self-pity, and suspicion (lack of trust) are present. These are the layers of self-doubt. As you document the areas, be sure to write down how this affects you and how it makes you feel for this is your reaction to the layers of self-doubt.

3. <u>Set goals</u>. Now that you have identified the areas of self-doubt and the associated emotions, take another week to write down action statements to turn those areas into venues of joy, forgiveness, humor, courage, hope, and self-confidence. The transformation must be founded in gratitude. This is the first step to removing the layers of self-doubt. Outline goals to match your action

statements. This is you identifying your range of work.

4. <u>Determine which goals you will pursue</u>. You know what work needs be done, but are you ready for change? Take a day to go somewhere quiet and peaceful. You may have a lot of goals and pursuing them all at once can be daunting. Use this day to determine which goals to pursue. This is you identifying what work you are willing to do.

5. Do the work! P.C. Cast said "I seek strength, not to be greater than other, but to fight my greatest enemy, the doubts within myself". Doing your work is you removing the layers of self-doubt. There are no excuses. If you get off track, you can always jump back on track! Remember to continue the gratitude journal. This is you filling in your new layers of self–confidence. You are on the beach in St. Lucia in a swimsuit...everyone can see you -the real you- and you are thrilled and comfortable with that.

12

Contagious Emotions

I began to think recently about what emotions I spread and what emotions I pick up from the people I interact with. When my son was little, I referred to him as Oscar (for Oscar the Grouch from Sesame Street) when he was in a foul mood. He disliked this because, in my opinion, it was a sign that I recognize and acknowledge his emotion. What if our friends did this to us – identified us by our emotions? Would we then be more aware? The first step to being aware of what emotions we are spreading is to be aware of our current emotions and to avoid denial of emotions. I am becoming increasingly aware of how my emotions impact the people around me. This awareness also helps me understand how others' emotions are impacting me.

So what are emotions? Jack Mayer describes emotions as the bridge between thoughts, feelings, and actions. Think about what is going on in your life right now. Notice the emotions you are exhibiting. There is probably a connection between the two. Do you feel fear, anxiety, depression, sadness, loneliness, shame, guilt, or frustration? Do you feel love, compassion, joy, contentment, happiness, or acceptance?

If you are struggling to identify your emotions, it is possible that you are busy suppressing them. The telltale signs of disconnected people may be someone who ignores the feelings of others, someone who pretends things do not happen, someone who abuses substances such as prescription drugs, alcohol, recreational drugs, or food, someone who is compulsive and/or excessive, someone who is consistently superficial, or someone who is too busy to feel. I am sure you could add some signs to this list as well. Whatever you are feeling should not be trapped or buried inside. Ask yourself if you operate out of fear or out of love. If you are unsure, ask a friend. Odds are they already recognize your emotions.

The truth is that hiding our emotions can make us tired and depressed. We may find ourselves overreacting to minor situations, walking about with a feeling of uneasiness, unmotivated, and unaware. If you think this will not affect the people you love, think again. "The more you identify with a person, the more likely you are to catch the emotion. Much of this occurs and we are completely oblivious to it" says John Cacioppo, Ph.D., Dir. of the Center for Cognitive and Social Neuroscience at the University of Chicago.

I challenge you to be more conscious and aware of your emotions. What are you spreading?

If you can access and be fully honest about the cause of your emotions, you can avoid passing them on to people who do not deserve it.

For example, if you have had a terrible day at work, you can refrain from passing it on to your children and spouse when you arrive at home. Become an expert at dissolving or diffusing your negative emotions. Try positive thinking techniques to transform into a more joyful and uplifting person. Doing this will make you more in tune with what emotions you are spreading and soon you will become someone people want to be around.

13

Controlling Self In A Passion Zone

Our abilities to control our emotions can TRANSFORM a day, a week, or even a year from sweet or sour. I have severed friendships, other relationships and even a marriage over what I believed to be a very controllable issue – the issue of controlling self in passion zones. In my personal life, I have found it important to NOTICE the areas which I am passionate about and the areas, things, or people which I CARE the most about. I discovered that these were the areas or "passion zones" that activated the most extreme inner emotions. They were the areas where I found myself acting out of someone's best interest or saying more than necessary or being noticeably expressive.

We all have these "passion zones" in our personal (including spiritual) and professional lives. I will describe some personal examples. Professionally, I really cared about saving the government resources, and I really cared about people being valued. When it appeared either of these were out of balance, I noticed verbal and physical changes in myself, and on occasion, I lost self-control. When I lost self-control, everyone around me knew it. Everyone knows when you lose it too.

Personally, I cared about my son and was willing to defend him at all costs. This created a zone of tunnel vision in which I could not see past his feelings enough to really decipher what was in his best interest. This resulted in a loss of my parental control and a degradation in my ability to take my parental responsibilities seriously.

Spiritually, I believed in the greater good and I still do! Believing this about everyone and everything seemed misplaced at times, but I have maintained this personal core belief. Let me describe this belief further. I believe that everyone can press on to greater things. I believe I have a responsibility to encourage others to never give up on life, on their dreams, on grandiose achievements. One area that I believed would help someone to PRESS ON was knowing the truth. I grew up with a father who was always brutally honest – or so I thought. What is so brutal about honesty? Honesty can be objective and subjective and sometimes its subjectivity makes it hard to swallow. Honesty up front can be better than a stream of lies. It allows one to correct their course much earlier and propels one towards success sooner.

The point is a loss of control in any area of 'self' can have either predictable or unpredictable consequences. A self-examination can REVEAL the circumstances driving this loss of control. Some will be self-inflicted, and some will be external. If you find it to be a circumstance outside of your span of control, then change your reaction. If it is a circumstance inside your span of control, then look at the benefit of changing the situation.

In the case of my work passion zone – government resource saving and person valuation, I chose a two-pronged approach: 1) listen longer before speaking, and 2) continue valuing others (practicing what I preach). In the way of valuing others, one specific action I took was to give people the benefit of the doubt more often (this did not always work out with my son). I chose to examine my role and the expectations of my level of involvement for each situation. This was a recurring dynamic process. I realized that not everyone needed my input and give the opportunity most people reached the same end state I desired without my inputs. Trying to relax and take deep breaths while listening in a conversation helped tremendously. I felt a hidden sense of personal accomplishment – no one knew but I was making small victories in the way of controlling SELF.

In the case of my personal passion zone – my son- I chose to listen to other inputs from people I trusted and cared about. I implemented ideas of others and watched the results roll in. In most cases, I was receiving sound advice and needed the alternative opinions to fill up my parenting toolbox. No one knew it but making the tough choices sometimes made me cry or made me sad but those emotions were an afterthought as my son continued to mature.

In the case of my spiritual passion zone – compassion - I continue doing a deep dive to examine how to insert compassion appropriately and frequently in my thoughts and actions.

Ask yourself - what are your 'passion zones', and how do you control yourself in these zones?

14

Identifying Negative Thought Patterns

Being aware of the energy you bring into the world can be achieved through thought observation. Thoughts drive actions in most cases. If you watch your thoughts which shape your mental state, you will realize that your thoughts form patterns that run through your mind throughout the day while applied to a variety of scenarios and situations.

When we find ourselves in a negatively charged situation, the natural and most common thing to do is to assign blame. By embracing "living in self", we can begin to look within and observe self.

We own the energy we bring into the world and take responsibility for it. Own your energy.

Negative thought patterns can be the foundation of unhappiness for ourselves and the people who surround us. Consider whether your attitude towards life is stopping you and others from bringing positive energy to any situation. To change the negative thought patterns most of us apply to life, we must first be aware of what they are:

- The OCD Thought Pattern: YOU are obsessed with perfection and constantly think that everything needs to be improved. Nothing is ever good enough.

- The Comparative Thought Pattern: YOU spend a lot of time comparing yourself to other people and as a result you always think you are not good enough.

- The Polarized Thought Pattern: YOU look at life as black or white – an inflexible view of the world. YOU fail to see the shades of grey present in nearly every issue or opinion presented to you.

- The Personal Attack Thought Pattern: YOU think that everything that does not go YOUR way is a cut against you personally.

- The Find A Problem Thought Pattern: YOU are always looking for problems or faults in any situation.

- The All or Nothing Thought Pattern: YOU do not give yourself or others an opportunity to live life in the grey zone. YOU feel that people's actions should always be "all or nothing" which makes failure a more likely outcome.

- The Envy Thought Pattern: You constantly envy those that are where you want to be in life and, as a result, you cannot be happy for them.

- The Overthinking Thought Pattern: YOU think too much about things instead of living in the moment. YOUR thoughts stifle you and prevent you from living.

- The Jump to Conclusions Thought Pattern: YOU constantly jump to conclusions without any evidence. YOU do not give people the benefit of the doubt.

- The If I Could I Would Thought Pattern: YOU make excuses for why you are not where you want to be instead of outlining the actions you will take to get there. As a result, YOU constantly feel powerless.

Now that you have identified what some of your negative thought patterns are, consider how continuing this type of thinking can negatively impact the people you interact with and how your actions might cause them to spiral into their own negative thought patterns or might bring them down.

Purging Your Mind of Negative Thoughts

Part of mental fitness is the process of putting positive, balanced thoughts into your mind. Sometimes we find this difficult to do if our subconscious has been conditioned to thinking according to negative thought patterns. The recognition that we might have faulty thinking and belief patterns programed into our subconscious can be a difficult realization. Think of the subconscious mind as the habit mind where all positive and negative habits are stored. These habits were programmed beginning with the day we were born. You may have 18 years of negative programming from your childhood or several years of negative programming from the use of an addictive substance or a bad relationship. If you do not take control of your habit mind, then you are choosing to let others control you.

*Make a conscious choice to transmit
and receive positive energy.*

For a period of 30 days, take steps to push the negative thoughts out of your mind by giving attention and focus to positive thoughts or positive affirmations. Continually disregard those negative thought patterns. Starve negative thoughts of attention and focus. Refuse your normal/old self. If necessary, focus on one thought pattern at a time and ensure you are not replacing the removal of that pattern with the introduction of another negative thought pattern. Consistency is one of the key factors for reprogramming/retraining the subconscious mind. Some of the most common ways of achieving increase positive thinking are:

- FOCUS: Focus on your thoughts and identify negative areas for removal.

- VISUALIZATION: Imagine positive states of being.

- MEDITATION: Quiet your conscious mind and then influence your subconscious mind.

- POSITIVE AFFIRMATIONS: Repeat positive statements to yourself for the purpose of installing new beliefs.

- CHANGE YOUR ENVIRONMENT: Change the people you hang around. Change the places you frequent. Change the music you listen to.

- CHANGE YOUR EATING AND SLEEPING HABITS: Poor physical health can negatively impact our mental state. Take care of yourself!

Watch your thoughts, they become words. Watch your words, they become actions. Watch your actions, they become habits. Watch your habits, they become your character. Watch your character, it becomes your destiny.

16

Getting Rid of the "Little" Mindset

Years ago, I visited two dear friends of mine – a married couple of over a decade. I am always interested in the interactions amongst married couples because I want to learn and apply lessons learned to my own relationship. The gentleman kept asking his wife to refrain from using the word "little" when she spoke. She would say "I have a little job" or "We have done a little bit to fix up this house" or "We're going to live on a little boat".

The word little means small, amount, or degree. The gentleman emphasized that throughout her whole life, his wife had minimized everything – her accomplishments, her worth, etc. In 2015, I cofounded the Wright Women Lean In Circle to focus on the empowerment and advancement of women at Wright Patterson Air Force Base. It turns out that this habit of minimizing accomplishments is quite common amongst women. When women are complimented, they tend to dismiss the accomplishment instead of embracing it.

When you listen to yourself talk, try to notice if you use words that minimize. Also try to notice if you use these types of words when you talk to other people to describe their efforts or contributions. Notice if you use the "little" word to describe your belongings. Notice similarly if you use the word "big" or any of its synonyms to describe what you perceive to be letdowns, mistakes or failures.

Words do matter. Our words are often a reflection of our thoughts. My advice is to look at your accomplishments with pride. If you cannot recognize each accomplishment as a significant step, then you may not progress to the top. Look at the things you have with pride and recognize that they are enough for you; your belongings do not need to be compared to other's belongings or minimized. Look at the seemingly negative moments (I call them life's lessons) and learn from them rather than dramatizing them.

Think of when you take medicine or when you bake something. The amount of medicine you take or the amount of the ingredients you use is not "little" or "big". It is "just right" for the recipe.

MAGNOLIA

The present need not be minimized or inflated. It is what it is and it should work for you.

Choose your words carefully. This big change (I almost said little!) will improve your self-esteem and make you much happier. Believe in self!

17

Picture Yourself There

In January 2016, I had an opportunity to visit a veterans' hospital. This turned out to be a rather thought-provoking experience for me. Some of the veterans that I visited with were completely mentally present and others were barely hanging on for life it seemed. Some could move about freely while others required a wheelchair. Some had all their limbs and others did not. Some simply rested during the visit and others talked. I wondered for a minute if I might end up somewhere like this when I got old.

The truth is the degree of quality with which we age and the speed at which we age is a big unknown. This reality further emphasizes living in the present. I sat for a long time next to a retired Lieutenant Colonel. I thought that while at one point he had a lot of command and power, now he was living at a veterans' hospital with few possessions surrounded by fellow veterans barely able to talk or move about. Some of the veterans had not served until retirement, but nonetheless, they had served and were afforded the same care as him. They all ate the same food and they all talked to the same people.

At the end, we all must die and this is a profound equalizer. The way we age may in fact bring us to the realization that we are better than no other human being sooner rather than later. When we are stripped of the ability to communicate in an articulate manner, walk, run, write, etc, what will we do?

Each day is truly a gift. Perhaps we can learn this lesson earlier in life and treat people as we felt compelled to treat these veterans in their last days - with compassion and gratitude.

18

Who Will You Be at 90?

The story of Patricia Davies struck me deeply. Peter Davies, now Patricia Davies, was a World War II veteran who lived a life publicly as a male for 90 years and privately as a male for 60 years. At the age of 90, she finally, after 87 years of secrecy, decided to publicly admit her transgender status.

How long will it take you to admit who you really are?

Do we live in a society that influences us to nearly die with our truths? Do our religions facilitate this closed mindset? Or is it our inherent selfishness that does not allow us to simply be happy for someone who has an unusual truth? While our governments or political parties may see cause to hold dear to old mindsets, we as individuals do not have to. What made people so uncomfortable with the idea of transgender for so long?

What is happiness worth to you? Would it not be worth the same to our friends and to strangers alike? What are the truths that define your core identity?

Read more about Patricia, my hero, at https://www.thesun.co.uk/news/3204144/world-war-2-hero-transgender-ninety/.

15 Minutes of Self Love

I created a simple beauty routine for myself because creating a habit of taking care of yourself is SO important. While this might be a physical habit, it has mental benefits. I am sure you have heard the adage - when you look good, you feel good. I could pretend I do not fall victim to low self-confidence from my physical appearance at times, but that would just be an alternative fact. I am going to be vulnerable and admit that I have had self-image issues over the years - some driven by my lack of love for myself which was exploited by people close to me and some driven by my desires to look a certain way. Over the years, I have taken steps to look the way I want to. Even still, there is pressure to cover up, to dress up, to undress more, to wear more makeup, to wear no makeup, to wear hair straight, wear hair curly, to wear shorter heels, flats, taller heels, etc. At the end of the day, we all just want to be accepted for who we are but an underlying vulnerability is present when we are not happy with who we are or when we succumb to the desires of others with regard to our appearance...and what about when we are threatened by the appearance of others or jealous of the appearance of others? If deep inside we are unhappy with who we are, then we alone must fix that and take the steps that result in self-love.

Taking ownership of our own happiness and being honest about our vulnerable areas is critical and overcoming our fears of changing and our fears of failure is the first step. Start with a simple routine...15 minutes of makeup, 15 minutes of exercise, 15 minutes of healthy eating, 15 minutes of cooking, 15 minutes of reading a good book, 15 minutes of playing a guitar, 15 minutes of self-love.

20

Creating A Personal Statement

For years, I have been trying to find words to describe a guy I dated named Travis and I have found it. Travis was a soul sinker. While on the outside he seemed to be trying to help me become a better person, he brought me down, way down. Travis went to great lengths to find out every detail of my past whether it was childhood memories, previous relationships, financial status, etc. Though this should have been a warning sign, I continued in this relationship. Travis examined my past in excruciating detail, piled my mistakes and failures on me, and continually humiliated me about my past. My past became a present nightmare where bits and pieces were thrown in my face. Travis just could not leave my past in the past. It is one thing to reflect on your past and the lessons you learned but it is an entirely different feeling when someone uses your past to humiliate you and make you feel like you are not enough.

Rather than focusing on the I AM, he focused on the I AM NOT. Think about that. Do you want people around you who constantly remind you of who you are not? I hope the answer is a confident NO. We should all strive to know who we are. Life is a lesson. Here is an exercise to try:

1) List ten I AM statements. Do this alone. No one else can say I AM for you. Think of your real genuine nature. What do you really believe about yourself?

- ✓ I am beautiful.

- ✓ I am confident.

- ✓ I am patient.

- ✓ I am peaceful.

- ✓ I am a great mother.

- ✓ I am a wonderful partner.

- ✓ I am well spoken.

- ✓ I am love.

- ✓ I am thoughtful.

- ✓ I am caring.

2) Create a personal statement that incorporates your I AM statements. The words you attach to I AM will find their way into your life.

I am a beautiful, confident, caring woman who is happy to be a wonderful partner and great mother. I am a patient, caring, peaceful, thoughtful, and well-spoken person. I am love.

3) Write your personal statement down on an index card. Speak or read your personal statement daily.

Sometimes it is fruitful to have healthy amnesia and forget about painful parts of our past and move on. MOVE!!!!

21

Your Happiness Is In Your Hands

I often hear people say "I want to be accepted for who I am". These people use this as a reason to make it acceptable to change me to facilitate their needs and wants. How does this work? Someone might be exceptionally nice to me by caring, sharing, and giving more than I give to them. Their self-imposed expectation of what my reaction to their niceness should be causes them stress. They begin to get frustrated that I am not doing what they want — they believe that if I do what they want, they will be happier. What should I do? Should I become aware of this expectation and accommodate it? Does it matter who the expectation is generated by?

I believe that I do not have the responsibility to make anyone personally happy. This is a SELF responsibility — it belongs to you and only you. I have the right to be myself. If you do not like it, move on. You have the right to be you. If I do not like it, I will move on.

MAGNOLIA

*You are responsible for your happiness. I
am responsible for my happiness.
Happiness resides inside you and I!*

I particularly felt this pressure in my relationship with my oldest sister. Every few months, we get in an argument about how I communicate or do not communicate with her. I do not meet her expectations, and this makes her feel unhappy. My relationship with her is not my primary source of joy. Therefore, not meeting her expectations does not devalue my spirit.

Something that can bind and restrict people is a feeling of obligation to maintain friendships and relationships particularly within their family. As children become adults, they feel pressure to continue pleasing their parents in a child-like manner and to continue propping up relationships with siblings and other extended family. Victims of abuse feel pressure to continue defending their abusers and continue prolonging a destructive relationship through this defense. They do this despite the resulting degradation of self and degradation of relationships with children, spouses, and friends.

You cannot make everyone happy, and you cannot make everyone accept you. You cannot expect others to bend over backwards for you and meet your expectations. We all fall into both categories to an extent. To that end, we can voice two statements: 1) "I am done jumping through hoops so you will like me" and 2) "I am done asking you to jump through hoops so I will like you".

Does this mean we are all done changing and going to remain stagnant? Absolutely not. Self-exploration, examination, and improvement are lifelong tasks. Keep moving forward but do stop trying to make others happy and burdening others by USING them as your primary source of happiness.

22

Protecting Self Esteem

I am thankful to no longer be surrounded by chronic and destructive criticism. Looking back, constantly expending energy to protect my self-esteem was exhausting over the years. Now I am free to pursue acts of compassion, happiness, self-love, and connections with positive friends and family. (2016 self-realization)

Now how did I come to be in a place where I had to protect my self-esteem and where negativity was a daily part of my life?

In my situation, I was romantically involved with an individual who was chronically critical and judgmental towards himself and others. I am not here to rehash all the ways he exhibited this behavior; generally, it seemed that fault finding was his behavioral pattern. I am here to learn from this experience and share those lessons with you.

To sustain a happy life, you must establish and then protect your self-esteem. I had to protect my self-esteem during these difficult times. Everyone must protect their self-esteem from the judgment that you and others impose provided they have established a sound and positive foundation of self.

At the time, I thought I had a healthy self-esteem but upon further examination, I had some work to do to attain an optimal level of self-love. Once I was no longer in this relationship, I felt free to be myself. Why did I stop being myself? In so many ways, I was trying to please someone else. While this can be an important mission, there is balance between pleasing someone and losing yourself.

To feel good about ourselves, we must stop the habitual criticism of self and others. This can be difficult if we are closely involved with someone who exhibits this behavior. Incidentally, this guy also thought that others were always criticizing him or looking down on him. This is what he did to others, and it was not true that everyone criticized him, or berated him, or wanted to somehow destroy him.

Eleanor Roosevelt once said, "No one can make you feel inferior without your consent." But that is easier said than done. Some of us learned as children to reaffirm what people told us about ourselves. If our parents criticized us all the time, we then thought what they said was true and perhaps that habit has migrated to adulthood without you realizing it.

Make negative (nonconstructive criticism) irrelevant to your self-esteem. There is a reason it is called "self" esteem. You must build yourself up! Every day, someone certainly can make us feel small, but we must strive to stop the permanent endorsement of negative labels and judgments. Stop watching others and critiquing them! Stop enabling others to exhibit this behavior towards you. If you exhibit this behavior towards yourself, commit to changing. Insert a compliment for every criticism until you break the bad habit.

Certainly, use constructive criticism and sound advice to become your best self. Surround yourself with people who drive you to be your very best. Do not be naive to the patterns in those you choose to surround yourself with. You can do this any number of ways, but I recommend writing as an effective way to remember experiences and to connect the dots.

5 Techniques for Emerging Successfully

without Desired Support

What happens when you are excited to embark on a journey and your family does not support you or even encourage you?

Your family and closest friends are the people you count on to be there for you no matter what. But sometimes, we must take some personal steps and do things a little bit differently when we are embarking on a new and positive journey.

1. Find a like mind. Seek out someone who is already doing what you want to do and ask them to be a mentor or adviser. At some point, this may turn into a friendship, but initially it just helps to talk to someone who knows what you are trying to do and can relate to it. They can be that positive sounding board you are looking for.

2. Check your reaction. Examine how you react to this lack of support and strengthen your inner core (your mind). Find a positive way to process the lack

of support such as meditation, working out, etc. Remember you can't control their response but you can control yours! You will emerge a stronger person if you can change negative inputs into positive outputs.

3. <u>Honor your intention</u>. Write your thoughts down. By the time you are done writing, you will be in a better space to move forward. This also allows you to track the trends in someone's behavior towards you and your reaction to their behavior. Finally, always write an intention for going forward at the end of each entry and try to keep this intention in mind for future interactions.

4. <u>Empower yourself</u>. Be decisive. Sometimes friends or family feel the need to help you decide and this can be confused with just supporting you. How many times have you told someone something and you just want them to listen instead of trying to always provide advice? Just decide and then discuss your decision. Make it abundantly clear what path you are on.

5. <u>Elevate your understanding</u>. Try to understand why the person is behaving the way they are. It may

have nothing to do with you and the sooner you understand that, the sooner you can frame their perspective as it relates to your journey. As a part of this, reflect on why you desire their support and if you really need it. Is a lack of self-love driving your need for support from others? Ask the hard questions. This understanding can help you change your approach to the important people in your life.

24

The Fear of Amazing

Andy Offutt Irwin said, "Don't be afraid to be amazing". Have you ever felt a sense of guilt when you accomplished something? It is the feeling that people are going to look at you with jealousy or with some sort of disdain due to your recent success. This feeling is usually followed by the act of downplaying your success. The fear of failure is often discussed more than the fear of success. Let us ask the difficult questions.

Will success make me less likeable? Will I be unable to find someone to love me once I become too successful? Will the ones that love me now be intimidated by my success? Am I worthy of success? Do I fear the thing that I want? Will people want or expect more from me when I become successful?

First, success is relative to you. You define your success. The act of comparative thinking is never good. When we compare ourselves to others, we cannot help but be dissatisfied. I once dated a guy who was always comparing my accomplishments to his and other's accomplishments to his and as a result, he always felt inadequate. There was nothing I could do about it. Even when I tried to celebrate with him a success he had achieved, it was always overshadowed by a comparison to someone else. At the same time, every time I had an opportunity to achieve something that required his buy-in or support, this boyfriend was the first to find a reason why I should not take the first step. After a while, it became an exhausting exercise in ego boosting. As a victim of comparative thinking by yourself and by others, your success becomes downplayed or envied, not celebrated.

Yes, it is true that when you do achieve personal success, some of your relationships will change. But you worked hard for your success. If those around you are unhappy about your success, that is their problem. Be present in your success and enjoy it.

Even feel free to share your success with others guilt free. The right person will feel motivated by your accomplishments, not intimidated or inadequate.

Self, Strength, Success

For some time, I wondered how the Live in Self initiative would assist me in my professional life. One week at work, I was fortunate to attend a Leadership Symposium where senior executive leaders come and share their experiences with growing into a leader and performing as a leader. An executive highlighted that the key tenet of leadership is knowing your inner self. All this time, I had been thinking that Live in Self needed to be a private endeavor of mine separate from my professional life! At the junior levels in the military, we are often encouraged to follow and discouraged from being ourselves because there is a fear that we need to grow into more mature selves that better align with our organizational values and vectors. I was encouraged and delighted that a senior leader had encouraged us to find ourselves and to then lead through honest and authentic expressions of ourselves.

Knowing others is intelligence; knowing
yourself is true wisdom. Mastering others

is strength; mastering yourself is true power. If you realize that you have enough, you are truly rich.

— Lao Tzu, Tao Te Ching —

Knowing yourself intimately means you are certain about who you are and what you stand for. It means you can state a personal vision, mission, and core values. What is the purpose for being able to state each of these? Your core values keep you grounded in your current words and actions. Your mission describes what you are doing today. Your vision describes where you are going.

This concept of understanding oneself can be executed through simplistic and older models such as the Johari window. When we look at the Johari method, there are four categories of self:

1. Known Self – things we know about ourselves and others know about us

2. Hidden Self – things we know about ourselves that others do not know

3. Blind Self – things others know about us that we do not know

4. Unknown Self – things neither we nor others know about us.

Having this level of self-awareness improves our understanding of our strengths. There are many processes and tools one can use to assist in strength identification. A recommended tool is the StrengthsFinder personality test. This can help us reflect on what our top strengths are and to begin the journey of increasing the probability for success in small and big endeavors. Some 360-degree feedback would also shed light on the hidden self or the blind self.

In the process of identifying our strengths, we also by default identify weaknesses which form our blind spots as we go through life. Another senior leader emphasized that, in general, people do not change a lot throughout their lives and as a leader, we should draw on what is within people. This is congruent with the idea that we are good enough just as we are. It opposes the idea that we should waste time trying to put into people what is not already there.

After we learn about our own strengths, a logical follow-on step as a leader is to learn about the strengths (and weaknesses) of people around us. When you know who you are, you can begin to look outward and empower people around you to reach their highest potential by utilizing their strengths.

The process of knowing oneself,
improving oneself (leading oneself), and
complementing oneself (looking
outward) is a marathon.

I realized that most highly successful people had learned early in their career about strength magnification and had been using this to propel themselves into experiences in which they thrived. Join me in running the course!

26

Healthy Anticipation

When you are pessimistic or assume the worst-case scenario, you construct a vision and world based on your expectations of the outcomes. When we expect terrible things to happen, we experience immediate discomfort or stress.

Anticipation results in the experience of expected future emotions. Therefore, if you must anticipate, anticipate positive endings, good health, success, positive beginnings, accomplishments, and blessings so that you can be present in a reality full of these things. Come to desire and expect the best outcome for yourself and others.

Anticipating pain was like enduring it twice. Why not anticipate pleasure instead?

— Robin Hobb—

MAGNOLIA

PART 2

FRIENDS, FAMILY, AND PARTNERS

Social fitness is building and maintaining healthy connections with others. In a world filled with electronic and physical interaction with others, it is so important to build and maintain trusted and valued relationships with family, friends and co-workers.

Growing up, I was not allowed to hang out with friends after school and on weekends. I never had the "birds and the bees" talk or the "dating" talk with my parents. I really began to learn about social norms when I attended the Air Force Academy, and even this interaction was constrained by having to stay on the base most of the time. At lot of my learning occurred through trial and error, and I forgive myself for the mistakes I made and try to take the lessons and have more meaningful social interactions today.

I know I am not alone. Many people struggle to establish and maintain effective and respectful communication with others. Our social status can often result in either a confidence boost or a mental state of depression or even a mental breakdown. Through our social fitness discussion, we explore how to gain and sustain healthy social connections and how to exhibit healthy social behaviors. We examine how to recognize personal strengths and which traits can strengthen the character of those around us.

1

It Is Not A Game

Shaun T. says in his famous Insanity workouts that "this is not a game; you have to dig deeper". Those words resonated with me and here is why:

We avoid conversations about fitness because they are uncomfortable. If we talk about it, we don't do anything about it. We avoid calling our eating and drinking habits the addictions that they are which we cannot break away from. We avoid working out because we might hurt ourselves. We hurt ourselves because we are overweight or out of shape. When we hurt one muscle we stop working out altogether using one hurt muscle as an excuse to let every other muscle lie conveniently dormant. I have done it. We have all done it. There are so many spoken and unspoken excuses we have all used.

We avoid working to become healthy individuals because it is inconvenient and unpopular. We are willing to let people influence our health who will not pay our medical bills or even take care of us when we get sick. We do this at the expense of the people who will share the cost of our medical bill and take care of us when we are sick or lose us prematurely because of our health conditions.

We sit around, eat happily and drink heavily around groups of people - friends, colleagues, business acquaintances, and even strangers because eating healthy is the unpopular choice.

Why don't we have the will power to make a different choice to embrace a healthy lifestyle even when it is unpopular? It is in our best interest and in the best interest of mankind.

It is time to stop making excuses. Dig deep. Be unpopular and change the mindset of your circle. I admire people who work out and people who try to eat healthy. I understand how difficult it can be and believe that they deserve to be admired, not envied.

2

Think Higher, Feel Deeper

When we say everything is possible, that means that both evil and good are indeed possible. Some people view their evil acts as a path to good. I bring this up in context of trying to explain the violence and the racism that has been highlighted recently but that has always existed throughout the world. We struggle to explain it. We also cannot explain atrocities such as the Holocaust and the Rwandan genocide.

What we can do is focus on individuals. We can focus on ourselves and, rather than looking outward, we can look inward to ask a few simple questions. Have I evolved? Have I learned? Why must we divide our species like this? What price does humanity pay for my thoughts and subsequent actions?

Eliezer Wiesel says we must always think higher and feel deeper. Where have your thoughts gone today - where do your thoughts go as you live? What do you do? The key is to simplify your thoughts and actions to small kind acts. Do not allow complicating thoughts to confuse you. You have a responsibility to simplistically act in manners that increase human survivability.

Start by simply speaking and acting like you care. The moments I look back on the most (with regret) are the moments where I communicated to someone that I simply did not care. And in that moment surely they thought, "Does she care? Does ANYONE care? The thought that you don't matter can lead you to think that you are invisible and that your memory is non-existent to others.

With the recent violent events in the news, one might notice that death has become a business for news agencies. Death is sensational, and everyone wants to have an answer, but what questions does the violence present YOU with? What do you ask yourself about yourself? Do you listen to the experiences of both sides? Do you watch the experiences of both sides? What do you choose to become a witness to? What do you claim as your answer? Do you engage in open discussion about the blatant indifference to anyone? Are you indifferent to others in your day to day experiences?

Are you indifferent to anyone - the drug user, the felon, the poor?

Human beings matter and we all bear witness to the experience of the human being. We can all be a little less demanding and a little more caring. Every moment is the beginning of something and we can choose in each moment to be a part of something good. We can think higher and feel deeper.

3

Keeping Others Safe

On December 26, 2015, I felt great empathy and sadness upon learning about the death of 28-yr old Marine Sgt. Tristan Clinger. After a long six days missing, his wife, parents, siblings, and three young children, along many comrades, friends, extended family, and complete strangers, learned of his fate. I worked with his father, a retired Master Gunnery Sergeant. My silent prayer for him was simply "Lord have mercy and bring you peace".

After a reported bout of depression, the thought of the military finding out about his struggle perhaps proved too much to bear. Being a combat veteran, I can certainly see how and why he may have wanted to keep this secret. In today's military, service members and veterans are encouraged to come forward and seek mental health for PTSD and other mental illnesses, but there is still much more work to be done as evidenced by the rate of military suicides. Every day over 22 Veterans and 1 Active Duty Soldier take their own lives.

The idea of deliberately smothering the life given to you

is seemingly incomprehensible to those who have not had suicidal thoughts before but then in a very present and real moment, it happens and cannot be undone. Is it the fear of feeling small and insignificant or the thought that we are no longer needed on this earth that causes the abandonment of the desire to live? Or is it the feeling of being overwhelmed by life itself? The pain must become truly too much to bear.

The suicide earlier that same year of Cara Miller along with the dialogues I had with two other military members who were suicidal this year made me think that the thought of suicide when it comes is subtle but then it becomes the only thought. I may never know or understand but these experiences more broadly have enhanced my understanding of the human bond. We are all connected. We are one. I heard Jimmy Carter once say that "on a cosmic scale, we are all in the same boat."

As I encounter people daily, I want to be a game changer. I want to change the trajectory of people's lives in a positive direction or enable people to maintain the positive track they are already on.

Certainly as a parent, I think a lot about the trajectory I am sending my children on. A small act now could result in much larger impact for years to come. Little did I know that my son would start communicating suicidal thoughts in 2016. I was completely unprepared to deal with this and I had to seek professional help for him that year as we battled his desire to no longer live. Through this process, I learned about many others suffering from either their own suicidal tendencies and thoughts or those of someone extremely close to them. I want to make people feel bright inside. What if we all consciously did this? In the profound words of Sydney Long, may we keep others safe from their darkness with our love.

4

Virgins and Shiny Lives

An email from a boyfriend:

You said that some days I try to tear you down and some days I'm really supportive. You said that I'm always looking for you to fail. The fact of the matter is we don't belong together. Nobody I know would have given you a chance, or if they had they would have used and abused you. I work really hard to build up your entire values system from scratch and try to share with you how I see an incredible relationship works. Not just an average relationship, but an absolutely incredible one. Very few women ever get the opportunity to be with a guy who will do so much for them or work so hard for them and love children and be capable of committing to them and avoiding strip clubs and other stuff like that. You are in a position many women would kill for. And you came into it with an incredible amount of baggage and with a history of making horrible and destructive decisions. You have one of the worst records with guys. I'm not looking for you to fail, or hoping you will fail. I want to succeed with you. But the fact of the matter is my risk analysis came up RED! I'm putting myself in an incredibly vulnerable position with someone whose history tells me they will fail epically. But I'm putting my heart under a guillotine anyway. Don't you think it would make sense to react strongly to signs that the blade was going to fall?

It really hurt when you got mad at me for being frustrated with having to raise you. You are like a child in so many ways and I am the father you never had in a lot of ways. That's not how a relationship is supposed to be. I felt horribly taken for granted so I explained to you in no uncertain terms why it is that I feel hurt on a daily basis and why I see you did not prepare for this relationship. It's like I have built up a relationship dowry of millions of dollars and all you have is an IOU. That sucks. But I work really hard to make it work. To try to see just the good in you that I know is there and become numb to the past. I am not an emotional person but in 30 minutes last night you completely turned my emotions upside down.

You dug your way into a dirty f--king little cave of pain and disgusting things and I am the only person who ever tried to help you. And last night you got mad at me for being frustrated about the fact that my woman was in that cave in the first place. But I stay! I stay here with you and hold your hand. I want to leave all of that behind and show you how happy and great the rest of the world is. I want you to bury your head in my arms and we will leave the place you made. I know what you have done. I know things about you nobody else does and I know how disgusting and horrible your life has been. I always wanted a virgin and a happy shiny life. But I won't leave you and I want you and I want you to be happy. It sucks not just being taken for granted but being attacked for having an emotional response to doing what I do for you. I don't get anything out of this. You don't pay me. I have never asked you for anything. I've never used you for anything. I just give to you endlessly. I give you time and caring and love and all those things you have never done anything to earn.

I hate saying that. I hate that it is the way that it is. I wanted a perfect happy little relationship but I can't have that with you. I have worked so hard to do the right thing. And last night I felt like you were attacking me for that. That sucks. But I won't give up. I won't leave. Not without you. I want you and I want to have a fantastic relationship with you and I have prepared for it and I work hard for it every day.

Well he did not stay. He gave me up for Lent. No matter how good most people think you are, there will always be those few, maybe just one person, who think you are red unmitigable risk. You must listen to their feedback, and then find another path where you can still grow without the harsh criticism.

The Gift of Fearlessness

Fear sucks. Too many times we either do nothing for fear of the outcome or we do something for fear of what happens if we sit still. Being bold, curious and aware makes me feel alive. I was determined to start my inner engine, get directions from my intuition, and head in the direction my curiosity pointed to. My map and the directions and turns along the way was only visible to me. Even as a little girl, people close to me felt that I was mysterious, unpredictable, and rebellious. This never died inside of me. Some admired this quality of mine and some feared it.

In the book The Pocket Chogyam Trungpa, the gift of fearlessness is described as a type of generosity. The gift of fearlessness is defined as reassuring others and teaching them that they do not have to feel completely tormented and freaked out about their existence. It is aiding others in seeing the basic goodness that exists in the world and aiding others in realizing that there is a way to sustain their life. I am reminded of people that I know that believe that their existence is continuously morphed in a negative manner by their surroundings and circumstances.

The truth is, to exist fearlessly, we must be willing to see ourselves. Do you look at yourself directly? Do you know yourself? Are you afraid of seeing yourself? Do you exist in comfortable frameworks as a method to avoid self-exploration? What frameworks allow you to "safely exist" without truly facing yourself?

In this moment, I face the side of myself that has struggled to manage my finances, the side of myself that sabotaged romantic relationships of mine and others, and the side of myself that has struggled to be fully engaged as a mother. Have you struggled in these areas too?

In my writing, I will often explore and admit parts of myself that are seemingly embarrassing. People often ask why I write about those embarrassing moments. When you do question these admissions, I would challenge you to tell me some part of yourself that you are embarrassed to admit. Use my admissions to generate bravery and courage within yourself to study who you really are. Unfold your habitual patterns that surround the lies you tell others about yourself. When you do this, you will begin to feel relieved. When you have faced the reality of life, you can start moving forward instead of moving in unproductive and lie-based perpetuity that has served you no good.

Now, I still believe that as humans, we all have a fundamental state of goodness within and we should certainly work to project this. I certainly see and appreciate the sense of goodness that emanates from so many areas of the universe. At the same time, we should not be condemned for our desires for the most part. But let us go BEYOND our fear and this is what is described as fearlessness.

Certainly, everyone wants you to be extraordinary, but it is good to be okay with being ordinary. Accept yourself just as you are and then use your imperfections as you progress and improve. Make them part of the journey.

Today, I give you the gift of fearlessness. Do not fear. Do not doubt. Do be courageous. Seek out an inner circle that gives you this gift, so you can study your truths in a safe environment and move forward in a positive direction.

Examining Our Circle

I went to a Santana concert recently with a friend. Santana said "Your mind is a magnet. You do not attract what you need or what you want; you attract who you are." I immediately felt a sense of gratitude for the friend that had so graciously invited me to the concert and began to reflect on the rest of my friends and professional associates. The phrase "you are the company you keep" kept playing in my mind. You can change friends as you transition from childhood to adulthood. As I have grown older, the company I have kept has either evolved or changed. Are we the company we keep? Who are we?

We must be present and aware to find out. Walk with me through a short mental exercise.

Examine you and your circle. Keep things honest here. You are doing this alone, and there is no need to lie to yourself.

- Think about the top five people you spend time with.

    o What are they like?

    o What do you like about them?

    o Do you want to be like them?

    o What have they enabled you to do over the years?

    o Do you look up to them?

    o Have your friends been the same for many years?

- Who are you?

    o What are your core values?

    o What principles drive your daily decisions?

    o How have you changed over the years?

If you do not like the answers to the questions, think about whether a change of scenery would be of benefit to you. When someone is doing something bad, people often recommend rehabilitation. In rehabilitation, one's scenery is changed. If one is not serious about the change, they leave rehab and return to their old routines. **You must want the change.**

Norman Vince Peale said, "Change your thoughts and you change your world." Do not underestimate the role that your company plays in your thoughts and ultimately your success. Bad company can paralyze your present and crumble your future.

You cannot have high expectations for your life and low consideration for your company.

Not sure of the character of a person? Then look at his or her friends. This is what many employers do when evaluating prospective employees. To some extent, your friends can define and influence who you are and where you are going.

You choose your company. There is a mutual acceptance of who we surround ourselves with and in some instances, both people are on different levels. Think of someone you really admire and then take notice of their inner circle. You are either elevating your friends or causing their decline. Your friends are either elevating you or causing your decline.

CHOOSE to surround yourself with people who believe in you, people who think, people who have vision, people who motivate you, inspire you, and push you in a positive direction. You choose!

Finally, **be the person you want to meet.** If you are friends with people who represent a desired end state for you, it is in your best interest to demonstrate positive and upward evolution. Otherwise, they may begin to think you are not worth their company.

When They Do Not Say I LOVE YOU

Maya Angelou once said, "When someone shows you who they are, believe them". I have heard Oprah add "the first time" to the end of this quote indicating that sometimes we take too long in the "believing" phase. At the beginning of my 2-year relationship with Travis, he communicated concerns that he had about my situation – about the unchanging situation of me being a divorced single mom whose ex-husband had visitation rights. At the end of my relationship with Travis, his concerns had not changed, and he took time to write some closing thoughts.

Regarding his efforts in the relationship, he always felt like he was doing too much, more than his best. Really, he did his best and at the end of it all, **love remained on the sidelines**. It never played. "I care about you a lot and always wanted to make you happy. I tried very hard to do so until the point where I realized that I could not emotionally do so without great cost to myself... the situation would not change so I found myself revisiting the same hurtful emotions….I did not leave you. Bhakti, it's not like that, I was forced out because I couldn't bear to stay. I think those are two very different things. It is not my fault that things are the way they are, and I wish that it were not so. I know that you made some extreme changes in your life after we met, and I am very proud of you for that. I feel bad that you did so much to change and I could not meet you from my side. To my credit, though, I did give up a lot of hopes and expectations and left many desires and expectations behind, which was very difficult for me. I just cannot go one more step. I need to be able to have an unimpeded future, and then I think I can forget the past. But it is so hard to forget when it's still in the present", he said.

Over two years of a committed relationship with Travis, he was hesitant to call me his girlfriend and never said he loved me. In fact, he felt forced out of the relationship by me. "I was forced out because I couldn't bear to stay" he said. He never accepted me as a divorced single mom whose ex-husband had visitation rights. He always thought that my son's future was bound for failure and he wanted an unimpeded future. The present was always clouded by the thoughts of a worst-case scenario future.

I cannot help but look back and think that Travis missed out on the present and on love. Love is not selfish. Love is about meeting someone in the middle. It is about not living in the past, enjoying the present and looking forward to the future.

I always wondered why it was so hard for my boyfriends to utter the **I love you** phrase. I spent many days doing so much to change. I do not regret that because it has shaped the woman I am today. The change was good. I am thankful that they did not utter **I love you** because I would have wrongfully assumed that they were also doing so much to change. In some of these cases, I was good enough, but the timing was not right. In other cases, I was not good enough in their eyes and the timing did not matter. When timing and acceptance both align, then something special is revealed.

I learned something else from this relationship — Travis knew when to walk away. Though we all hate giving up, we should recognize the moments when something is in fact dead and make the choice to not let the situation control us. Sometimes space and time gives us a chance to remove the rose-colored glasses and see things clearly. When something is dead, just leave it. In time, you will know whether you have made the right decision.

8

Past, Present and Future Viewpoints

Some time ago, I was approached by then ex-boyfriend Travis whose current girlfriend had recently been diagnosed with a popular sexually transmitted disease (STD) named Human Papilloma Virus (HPV). Travis thought it was appropriate to contact me to inform me of the finding and to investigate whether I had anything to do with the situation.

He found himself in a conundrum that he had never expected being a virgin himself. I relayed to him all the information that I knew about HPV and discussed with him the results of my annual STD tests, none of which indicated that I had the STD. Travis had never had annual STD tests – after all perhaps he thought they were not necessary for someone who maintained physical contact with girlfriends while being a good Catholic boy and refraining from actual sex. Unfortunately for him, even annual tests probably would not have detected the HPV if he had it. It would be almost impossible to pinpoint where his then divorced girlfriend had contracted the disease.

One thing was for sure: It was not my problem. Possibly disappointed that I had no self-blaming news for him, Travis then said, to me "I cannot change what has happened, but I have to make decisions as to how to handle things in the future. You know I over think things. I am a very intelligent person and I am very good at solving engineering problems because I over analyze things and examine them from many perspectives and calculate the worst-case scenario. That same ability can be very debilitating in relationships...and that results in loss of sleep and eventually depression which can become severe. Luckily, I have moved to a new job, so I have that to cling to. I have been working long hours so that I can focus on work and not think about other things. If you do not worry about the future enough, you live in the now and make poor decisions that negatively affect your future options in life."

I have often pondered...if we go through life over examining things and calculating the worst- c a s e scenario, will we be successful or even happy? This is a very risk adverse approach; some view it as cautious and thoughtful. In this case, Travis chose to continue this approach at his job and to avoid his relationship because he found his job to be an environment where he could succeed. This made sense for his job — you would not want a bridge builder to not consider the worst-case scenarios when building the design! At the same time, if you thought of the worst-case scenario for driving down the freeway, you would never drive anywhere. If you thought of the worst-case scenario for any friendship or relationship, you would never enter one.

Travis found it challenging to change his approach when entering relationships. He still sought to analyze emotions when that did not always result in the fruitful engineering solution that he had hoped for and, as he admitted, the results were debilitating. He was miserable, and it was all within his control!

I have always thought that, in life, a balance needs to exist. This communication with Travis gave me some closure and allowed me to understand and validate what our relationship had been about.

Being a divorced single mother, my relationships were always a challenge in interesting ways. In some cases, when two people begin a relationship, if both are virgins, or both are childless, or both have not been previously married, there is a naïve sense that there is also no baggage to deal with. A certain degree of maturity is required to learn to maneuver in a relationship where some serious baggage is brought in...and make no mistake...baggage is always there. Sometimes I thought I might be better served to avoid relationships all together. The tendency to overanalyze relationships can be debilitating but the appropriate balance of this quality is good.

Travis also believed that my life and the life of my son was probably doomed to fail because I had failed to consider or worry about the future when I decided to marry my first husband after only knowing him for five days. He was right about one thing; I did fail to fully consider everything prior to jumping into a marriage. This marriage resulted in the birth of my son, and this single event -the birth of a child- has been a primary driver in my life decisions since. I choose to live a life where I do not look back and see a reflection of my future in my past. Worrying about the past or the future can paralyze one into inaction. I am looking into my present and my future, and I love what I see!

My lesson is: It is important to live in the present and understand how present decisions can shape our future. This does not mean worry though. It means be aware. AWAKEN. BE. Do not live in a tunnel....and if you do, try to avoid tunnel vision. See the light as often as possible. If you make a mistake, learn and keep moving!

9

Do Not Be Afraid Of The Breakup

Have you ever said to yourself, "I want to find anything to do but be present with myself." Have you ever thought something along these lines? These were words that I said after a particularly difficult breakup. Unbeknownst to me, I had been given up for Lent by a guy I had been seeing. I know what you're thinking – did that happen? Yes, it did! Over a period of a month, I wondered what I had done to result in no contact from someone I had cared about for two years. Following Lent, the guy told me that he could no longer be in a relationship with me.

I took a week-long sabbatical in Kauai, Hawaii alone. During this time, I felt too vulnerable to interact with anyone, even close friends and family. I needed the time to clear my head of all the negativity that relationship had brought me. It was a definite sign that this relationship was the last thing I needed. In those post breakup days, I found that being alone was depressing but necessary. I had to learn that the misery (or freedom) of being alone was better than the misery or imprisonment of the relationship. It was a process that I needed to ENDURE. Sometimes when you are going through something like this, time will heal you. You must see the process through; most importantly, do not ignore and avoid the pain.

I can admit now that I was not strong enough or willing to part ways when the relationship was clearly not right for me. Deep down, I still thought that I should be able to and could make any relationship work. Even though previously I had been divorced after hastily and carelessly entering a marriage with the same train of thought, I had not learned my lesson. Luckily, there was a breakup brewing on the other side and for that I am thankful. **Sometimes it does not matter what the escape route is or whether it is planned by you...all that matters is that you get out.** Today, I would be happy to thank Travis for breaking up with me and for doing it in a manner by which I could not drag out the breakout emotionally.

Years later, I left my fiancé and used these lessons to 1) not fear the breakup and 2) cope with the breakup in a positive manner. Many people thought

MAGNOLIA

I had gotten over the relationship too quickly, but really, I had just done my work.

10

Let Go Of Your Story

If you have been around veterans at all, you will notice that they tell a lot of stories, reminiscing on places they went, missions they were a part of, people they encountered, etc. Veterans often miss the good ole' military days, the military people and the military atmosphere. They often struggle to "reintegrate" and to find contentment in a non-military environment. Many people that I talk to who are having trouble living in the present are constantly talking about "their story". I realized today that hanging onto our story can be crippling. Throughout much of my life, I have carried most of my stories inside, especially ones I felt embarrassed, guilty, or shameful about. Many of them are buried deep. I developed a coping mechanism as a small girl of forgetting experiences (and associated feelings) that I did not like or did not want to remember. This mechanism later resulted in my forgetfulness of happy encounters as well. As such, the details of much of my life are lost. Over time, I have found that not living in many of my old stories consciously or subconsciously allows me to see the here and now with increased clarity. Other times, I feel like I am just passing through. I still have many stories. Today I encourage you to **LET GO OF YOUR STORY**. Hanging onto our story is often self-serving with the intention of keeping the world focused on us when we should really be focused on service to others.

In 2014, I was blessed with a beautiful niece, Valene Beloved. Valene is beautiful, strong, and innocent. Her stories are starting to materialize. At birth, we were all envisioned with infinite worth, original beauty and goodness, and we had no story at that instant. Life was simple in that moment. It can be simple and beautiful again if we let go. Some of the stories we tend to remember the most are negative. Denise Kirkman says "we are a people who have been defined by our oppressors and we continue to use this skewed prism to measure our worth". I often find myself discussing "what I have been through", but it is not this story that defines my worth. Rather, it is how I conduct myself today.

I had the privilege of going to Muir Woods and while there I was able to see the giant sequoia trees that are hundreds of years old. No one thinks about how they grew over hundreds of years – we all just look at the result in awe – we look at their current state. It is today's result that matters.

If I have a "Donald Sterling moment", no one will care about any story I have. Donald Sterling was a financially successful businessman (billionaire) who many people had never heard of until his racist comments to a mistress were released to the news media and went viral. Sterling was a long-time NBA team owner with a dismal record of losing. In that moment, the spotlight focused on how the NBA should punish him for his off-color disparaging comments. No one cared about his "story" and his "path to success". They cared about what he had done in that present moment. Now he will have to figure out how to let go of his story and live in his present.

That brings me to another realization. If it is true that we should let go of our story, then we should probably follow the golden rule and let go of others' stories. This does not mean to forget – letting go and forgetting are two different things. Remember, as hard as this is to do, it never hurts to see the good in someone. You can ALWAYS see the good in someone if you choose to. If you want to forget your story, then honor others and do the same for them. Today is a brand new day, and my story is the present moment.

11

Is Your Best Good Enough For Others?

The brownBerry books are about self-inspection, self-exploration, and self-improvement in all areas of our lives whether that is spiritual, physical, or mental. I think it is great to maintain a few friendships with people who cause you to look inward and speak to the nature of self, that is: your self. Chances are that none of us are perfect today. Listen to what people say and learn. Even if you do not like them, listen and learn.

Shortly after my breakup with Travis, I posted a pointed social media status that said "I shouldn't be sad that you're gone. Hell, you never arrived!" Travis contacted me and said that I had hurt his feelings. He said, "I did arrive. I threw caution to the wind and jumped into your arms with both feet. It didn't end how I had hoped but I honestly can say I gave it more than my best shot, more than I could afford to give. I'm sorry it is what it is but I really did my best. Please do not hate me because my best is not what you wanted." First, I do not think it is possible to give something "more than your best shot", but I do believe that people give their best and that their best is dynamic. Believe in the greater good and give others the benefit of the doubt.

Travis hit the nail on the head: Do not hate someone because their best is not what you wanted. This does not mean that you should allow yourself to be continually taken advantage of though. Recognize when their best is good enough and when it is not. I rarely had a bad breakup in all the flings, short and long relationships I have had. I considered my breakup from Travis to be my worst, but I learned that it was improper to hate him for his best. I carried this lesson to future relationship breakups and as a result, I do not dislike any ex-friends or ex-boyfriends. I do truly wish them the very best experience for their lives moving forward. The best thing to do was to learn the lessons from the experience and move on.

12

Consumption of Difficult People

My thoughts on difficult people are very succinct, so I will just get right to the point! I would like to think that by focusing on our inner self, we can solve a lot of our own personal issues, but sometimes, an external force seems to hinder our ability to focus on self. I have people in my life that are so toxic – their energy alone is enough to send me into a state of anger and frustration. We all know "that person".

Do you know someone who is the voice of doom and gloom, someone who knows it all, someone who ensures most things center around them, someone who is better than everyone else, or someone who is always dramatic? Remember that this person is simply expressing externally what is present internally – a void. Void means empty, bare, or unfilled. What if your pantry was in this condition? You might feel as if you have no nourishment – that you cannot survive. Your body would enter survival mode.

Difficult people are precisely that – they always seem to be in survival mode – the roof is always falling and they are always trying to find someone to save them, to make excuses for them, to live under the weak leaky roof with them. Perhaps they feel hurt, perhaps they feel insignificant, perhaps they feel wronged or perhaps they feel like they are being ignored. Whatever the case, this person generally lacks something inside to ground themselves, and being the voice of doom and gloom, knowing it all, being dramatic, etc., makes them feel important and noticed.

Do not let the difficult person consume your life. When you cannot avoid them, try not to get upset with them or to control or change them – this is simply a fruitless waste of energy. Rather, be neutral and exercise love (tough love is ok too) and patience when it is necessary to be in their presence. Most importantly, keep them on the surface of your psyche, not allowing them to penetrate your defenses nor consume the precious space surrounding your soul – do not allow them to be a part of your being, your identity, your self.

13

Are You Identified By Skin Color?

When my son was in 2nd grade, I took him to a classmate's birthday party at Laser Quest. There happened to be two children named Alessandro in my son's 2nd grade class. At the start of the school year, the teacher seemed to struggle with how she would tell homework apart so I always ensured my son wrote his last name on his school work.

I was aware that other people differentiated between them by saying "Alessandro O." and "Alessandro K." which I found to be appropriate and acceptable. While at the Laser Quest party, another parent (let's call her Suzy) approached me to say hello. I had seen Suzy before but had never had a particularly personal conversation with her. Suzy began to tell me that her children often talk about "Alessandro" at home and when asked "Which one?" by her, they differentiated by using the terms "the peach-skinned Alessandro" and "the brown-skinned Alessandro".

I had never noticed a color difference between my son Alessandro and the other Alessandro. So, I became rather inquisitive and learned that my son was the "brown-skinned Alessandro". My son is of German, Icelandic, Guyanese, and Argentinian heritage. The other Alessandro is at least partially Peruvian and Italian. I am unsure of the other elements of his ethnicity.

I uncomfortably ended the conversation with Suzy. I began to think, "Does skin color matter?" and "Why do we feel the need to identify people by their skin color?" I began to recall my experience of growing up in Hattiesburg, Mississippi where racism was still very much alive in the 1980s and 1990s. I remembered being told by my teachers that I HAD to pick EITHER "black" or "white" on standardized tests. Race was mutually exclusive. There were no other options. I thought to myself, "My mother is of a light complexion (German & Icelandic) and my father is of a dark complexion (Guyanese). Why do I have to pick just one of those when I am in fact both?" It seemed wrong.

As time went on, more options were sometimes present on national level standardized test forms such as the SAT or ACT. That is just one simple example. I also remember struggling with my identity because from the outside, I was just another "black girl", but the reality was that I also had 50% German/Icelandic as well. Since I HAD to pick ONE, I thought "why cannot I pick the white half of me?" and "wouldn't I be equally justified in selecting white as my race?" I recall the "one drop rule" – a historical term in the United States for the social classification of Negro as individuals with any African ancestry – a person with one drop of Negro blood was considered black. This was adopted as a statute in 10 states between 1910 and 1931. Children of mixed unions were invisibly black.

My association with being identified by race is negative. My mother's parents even disowned her for many decades due to her marriage to a colored man. They feared she would have inferior and subpar children. It is difficult to comprehend being labeled as such prior to even being born or even as a baby. I imagine for people who have these thoughts, the reality of a minority President must be difficult to comprehend.

Let us think if we have ever seen a "black" or "white" person. Societal standards for identifying a person as black or white do exist. Identifying someone by their color is a derogatory uninformed way of defining someone's perceived ethnicity in my opinion. Stephen Quintana states that "the term 'ethnicity' is contrasted with race in that the connotations of the former refer not specifically to physical, biological, and genetic features but to primarily sociological or anthropological characteristics, such as customs, religious practices, and language usage of a group of people with a shared ancestry or origin in a geographical region".

It seems easy and natural to reference someone's skin tone as "black" or "white" in casual conversations but most people rarely stray outside those colors. Either way, adding someone's skin tone does little to add value to most of these conversations – neither does adding height, eye color, shoe size or any other qualifier.

In the case of Suzy, she had resorted to "brown" and "peach" in her house as the way to distinguish between two children named Alessandro. There were many other ways she could have chosen but this seemed to be the simplest for purposes of conversations between her and her children. While Suzy and her children probably meant no harm in their distinction, I wish she had not allowed her children to be so drawn to the color of my son's skin but rather to other distinguishing characteristics.

Alessandro K.'s mother shared with me later that in her culture, it was strange to identify people by color. She said that when she came to the United States, it was odd to her that people were identified so often by the color of their skin. In her culture, it was common to identify animals in this manner but NEVER people. She was very disturbed by the conversation we had with Suzy.

In our quest to become socially fit, it is important to be cognizant of these sensitivities.

For more on Children's Developmental Understanding of Ethnicity and Race, read Stephen Quintana's Work at http://global.wisc.edu/multiracial/docs/quintana1998.pdf.

14

Life Lessons on Breakups

When you have a close friend going through a breakup or you are going through one, it can be a very confusing time. Most people experience at least a couple of breakups during their lifetime. It can be difficult to transition from the "time to love" period into the "time to let go" period. During the "Let Go" period, we can experience very intense emotions, but remember that the end of the relationship does not have to be the end of your world. Letting go in the right manner can and will prepare you for all that awaits you – all the love and all the good. To let go effectively, we must learn strategies for enhancing our mental, physical, spiritual, and emotional hearts. Here's some tips to help us all along during a breakup.

Do not engage in long periods of self-blaming. Often in a breakup, the other person blames you for the failure of the relationship. While we all have our roles and parts to play in a relationship, know that you must have a strong self-esteem prior to dating. If put-downs are sticking to you, you are not ready to be in a relationship. Be established in your own regard, and remember that it is not your job to fix who someone is at their core.

In many of my previous relationships, I lacked self-esteem and was often led to believe that I was not worthy of a relationship — instead I was worthy of a superficial, one-level deep, on their terms, physical relationship. Now that I am on more solid ground, I can vehemently state that I am worthy of so much more!

<u>Do allow yourself to feel the true emotions.</u> Accept that the breakup is real and has happened — write down any feelings you have that you are unwilling to share with others. Drowning yourself in alcohol or other addictions slows you down and intensifies your negative emotions. Heal without the aid of substances like alcohol and drugs. Allow yourself to take your mind off the breakup in healthy nondestructive ways — focus on eating healthy, getting good nights' rests, and exercising regularly. Remember that "this too shall pass". The feelings of a breakup are TEMPORARY and you will SURVIVE and OVERCOME.

In most of my previous relationships, I did not seek out drugs or substances to help me drown out the feeling of pain and some part of me believed that I would survive and overcome. I did however suffer from a lack of sleep. A breakup would set me into a spiral in which I would sleep only a few hours each night. Eventually, I drove myself to exhaustion.

<u>Do not stay in touch with your ex</u>. Once you know the breakup has occurred, make a clean break and take significant time apart to allow your emotions to cool. Contact simply lengthens the healing process. Do not make up excuses to contact your ex. Do know that it is better to be alone with the potential to be happy than to be miserable and unsatisfied in a relationship. If you are meant to be friends with your ex later in life, allow that to happen naturally.

In most of my previous relationships, I stayed friends with my exes and, in my mind, there was always a gate for reopening the emotional and physical gateways that I held the key to. Most of these gateways are superficial, artificial, and self-destructive and this mindset was not conducive to the ability to give fully to present and future relationships. Over the years, most gateways were closed by marriage to another partner. Even still, I found my exes wondering how I was doing and wanting to know that everything had turned out ok. Perhaps I was their 20%. Unfortunately, 20% was not enough to create a sustainable loving relationship in the moment. Most of them do not wonder any more.

Do stay in touch with close friends. It is necessary to have friends that you can check in with regularly. Lean on friends that will uplift you and support you whenever you are feeling an urge to contact your ex. Recognize that continuing to rely on an ex for emotional support only deepens the wound.

In most of my previous relationships, I would shut out the world during the breakup. After one particularly difficult breakup, I took a 10-day trip to Hawaii alone. I wanted to wallow in my sorrow alone, and this prolonged the breakup period significantly. If I had reached out to friends during and after the relationship, I would have had the support structure necessary to save myself from some serious and seemingly never-ending pain.

<u>Do allow yourself time to mourn your loss.</u> Express your true emotions. Allow yourself to cry, be angry, and release unpleasant emotions for a limited period. Try to seek out people and activities that will put you in a good mood.

In most of my previous relationships, I did allow myself time to mourn but it was not for a limited period – it was for an indefinite period. I felt as if the pain would last forever. Eventually I started approaching a new relationship with the idea that there was an inevitable pain that would occur. To alleviate this, I would create an imaginary idea of what the new person would be for me – and of course, they always represented perfection. For better and worse, I wrote my own destiny.

<u>Do see the truth and the realities.</u> Be honest with yourself. Allow yourself to see the flaws in the relationship. Do not continue defending your ex for their misgivings. Take one day at a time and focus on the present. Looking too far into the future can delay your acceptance and moving on period.

Amid considering a divorce, an acquaintance advised me to "do my homework". The homework was to identify all the good and bad of the relationship in writing. When I did this, the acquaintance showed me that most of the things on my list in the bad column were things I could not change, and I was operating in or below the 20% threshold area. The "threshold idea" is that we can generally find someone who meets 80% of our expectations and we can either spend the rest of our lives looking for someone who has the missing 20% or we can be happy in our present with the 80%. The 80% is obviously better.

The truth is that we ignore most problems in a relationship with the hope and belief that as the relationship grows, we will overcome these issues together – but people cannot be changed that easily, if at all. It takes two whole people (80%s) to make a relationship work over a sustained period.

<u>Do not find a new partner immediately</u>. Take time to heal and do not enter rebound relationships. There's always someone on the fringes waiting for you to breakup with your partner so they can get their chance. Just take your time deciding who to be with next. Give every potential partner a fair chance to receive what he/she truly deserves – your

undivided focus. Allow yourself time to learn from the mistakes of your last relationship and to refocus on the characteristics and qualities you really want in a partner. Have a healthy relationship with SELF. Cater to your wants and needs, find new hobbies, make time for new friends and old friends, and put yourself in a position of higher confidence.

In previous relationships, I either maintained new partners on the sideline or found them immediately after a breakup. These relationships always failed because I was never fully available. As such, I also tended to attract partners who were not 100% available either. I also frequently confused attraction and attention with love. I fantasized about being the Olivia Pope to Fitzgerald Grant, and I was on many occasions. Those relationships were designed to fail from the start. It was not until I decided to be 100% available to my partners and to expect the same in return that I found a partner fully committed to me.

<u>Do live in your season</u>. The keyword here is "IN". For everything, there is a season. Immediately after a

breakup, you enter the season to hurt but eventually you must move on.

I love the phrase "live and learn". My life changed when I realized that every experience, rather than being viewed as a mistake, could be instead a vehicle through which I learned. That's right — experiences are lessons — they are life's teachers. As I maneuver through life and use each experience to teach me, I prepare and mold myself to experience the present and future in ways I had never imagined possible.

15

Associations and Friends

Tina, a college classmate and friend shared the following insight with me in 2008. It was great advice that I am happy to share with you today.

The less you associate with some people, the more your life will improve. Any time you tolerate mediocrity in others, it increases your mediocrity. An important attribute in successful people is their impatience with negative thinking and negative acting people. As you grow, your associates will change. Some of your friends will not want you to go on. They will want you to stay where they are. Friends that do not help you climb will want you to crawl. Your friends will either stretch your vision or choke your dream. Those that do not increase you will eventually reduce you.

Consider this: Never receive counsel from unproductive people. Never discuss your problems with someone incapable of contributing to the solution, because those who never succeed themselves are always first to tell you how. Not everyone has a right to speak into your life.

You are certain to get the worst of the bargain when you exchange ideas with the wrong person. Do not follow anyone who is not going anywhere. With some people you spend an evening: with others you invest it. Be careful where you stop to inquire for directions along the road of life. Wise is the person who fortifies his life with the right friendships. If you run with wolves, you will learn how to howl.

In prosperity our friends know us; in adversity, we know our friends. If you associate with eagles, you will learn how to soar to great heights. The simple but fact of life is that you become like those with whom you closely associate – for the good and the bad.

Do not be mistaken. This is applicable to family as well as friends. Yes...do love, appreciate and be thankful for your family, for they will always be your family no matter what. Just know that they are human first and though they are family to you, they may be a friend to someone else and will fit somewhere in the criteria above.

The Power and Divinity of Forgiveness

Not forgiving will cost you your well-being – physically, emotionally and spiritually. What if I told you that forgiveness allows us to take responsibility for our own happiness AND forgiveness is an act of strength and divinity?

> *The weak can never forgive. Forgiveness is the attribute of the strong.*
>
> — Ghandi —

You have the power to forgive – sometimes you do not want to! Some of us need to be convinced that the act of forgiving is more powerful and beneficial than choosing not to. Hating is a choice. Remaining a victim is a choice.

> *Forgiveness has nothing to do with absolving a criminal of his crime. It has everything to do with relieving oneself of the burden of being a victim–letting go of the pain and transforming oneself from victim to survivor.*
>
> — C.R. Strahan—

One might say that feeling resentment and having negative thoughts about those who did harm to you is the natural way to respond to such things – but this does not make it the BEST way. Is your present happiness more important than your past suffering?

When you choose to hate or choose to harbor resentments, you forget how to gift yourself. Forgiveness is a gift we give ourselves – it is part of our inner power! It does not change what has happened, but it ensures that we can move into a state of happiness with peace of mind. To have peace with something is to have control over it. Recently someone said to me "Not forgiving is like drinking poison and expecting the other person to die." I have also often heard that "when you fail to forgive, the only person who suffers is you".

Harness your inner strength. Start with the small things. Make forgiveness a habit. Release the negative tie between you and other people and stop focusing your energy there. Become free by focusing on the good.

MAGNOLIA

Forgiveness is not an occasional act, it is
a constant attitude...we must develop
and maintain the capacity to forgive.
He who is devoid of the power to forgive
is devoid of the power to love. There is
some good in the worst of us and some
evil in the best of us.

— Martin Luther King—

Sometimes to harness a power, we must be humble. Being humble does not mean being weak. When your ego rules, forgiveness can be a very unattractive thing. Strive to be humble. And if you do not want people to know you are humble, that is ok – forgiveness can happen privately.

I wondered if that was how forgiveness
budded; not with the fanfare of
epiphany, but with pain gathering its
things, packing up, and slipping away
unannounced in the middle of the night.

— Khaled Hosseini—

It is an internal healing. Forgiveness heals the guilt and the hurt, and it does this quietly, privately, and thoroughly.

Forgive yourself and others fully knowing that God never needs to be asked twice.

To err is human; to forgive, divine.

— Alexander Pope —

Forgive fully. Give up hope of a better past. If you want complete peace of mind, you must let go of all grudges and resentments.

If you let go a little you will have a little peace; if you let go a lot you will have a lot of peace; if you let go completely you will have complete peace.

— Ajahn Chah —

Think about the Golden Rule. Then ask yourself if you have ever hurt someone without the intention of hurting them? Try this thought – The majority of people are doing the best they can with what they know, with where they are and with what they've got. What goes around comes around. By trying to hurt the one who has done you harm, you will likely fall into the same level as he did and move into a vicious cycle of lose- lose situations.

Remember to live mindfully. Use seemingly negative experiences as opportunities to learn and become better. Humanity is your teacher. Perhaps, it is time to remove some people from your life who are not here for your highest good or a greater good. Hurtful situations can provide opportunities to practice self- love. If you truly love and accept yourself, then it is very difficult for people to bring you down. When someone close to you begins to treat you badly, use the situation as a catalyst to become more self-reliant. Use the situation in which you feel hurt to learn, grow, and become that stronger better person.

To forgive is to set a prisoner free and
discover that the prisoner was you.

— Louis B. Smedes —

Ever noticed how bitter people seem to be surrounded by other bitter people? When you are an enjoyable person, you will attract more positive people. Be known for WHO YOU ARE — for being fa kind forgiving person is a sure way to attract others with similar qualities.

Do not take life so personally – remember that humanity is your teacher – humans are imperfect and we all make mistakes. Whatever people say or do or whatever people do not say or do not do is not about you – it is ALWAYS about them.

Show your willingness to forgive those who have hurt you and then people whom you have hurt will be more likely to forgive you. On the way to forgiving others, do not forget to accept responsibility for your actions and forgive yourself. When you forgive fully, you will feel better, be healthier, and be more enjoyable. What are you waiting for? If you still feel like you are not ready to forgive, then at least set the intention to forgive in motion – open your heart to the possibility of forgiveness. Be "that guy".

Be the one who nurtures and builds. Be the one who has an understanding and a forgiving heart one who looks for the best in people. Leave people better than you found them.

— Marvin J. Ashton —

Make the following statement of self-intention: I will be humble. I will give up hope of a better past and focus on a better future. I will forgive generously. I will offer forgiveness quickly and I will apply forgiveness freely. I will express it graciously and I realize that forgiving allows me to keep progressing. I know that majority of people are doing the best they can with what they know, with where they are and with what they've got – this includes me. I choose freedom and strength by using hurtful situations as a teacher. I choose to forgive fully.

17

Making Social Media A Positive Experience

The more some people use social media, the worse they feel. I felt compelled to write about this topic because I believe that the use of Facebook degrades many peoples' mental health. Baroness Greenfield, professor of pharmacology at Oxford University, believes that Facebook has created a generation of people who are obsessed with themselves, have short attention spans, require instant gratification, and have a childlike desire for constant feedback on their lives. This behavior leaves people with an identity crisis – their definition of being or self is shaped by people knowing about their feelings and activities. Are you one of those people?

First ask yourself some questions:

- Does social media negatively affect your self-esteem?

- Does social media validate you?

- Do you compare yourself to others on social media whether that is through comparison or weaknesses or achievement?

- Do you feel strongly about whether your posts are liked or commented on?

- Does social media make you feel that people around you are living trouble-free, perfect lives?

- Do you check social media multiple times each day?

- Does social media make you worry about what people think of you more than what you think of yourself?

- Are the relationships you nourish on social media shallow or meaningful?

- Do you "sell yourself" to others on social media? Do you get an emotional high when someone likes or comments on the things you post?

If you answered yes to a few of those questions, keep reading. There are 5 things you should avoid using social media for:

1. Do not use social media to compare yourself with other people. This can produce an inferior feeling in yourself.

2. Do not use social media to seek attention. This results in increased frustration from having fewer comments and likes when compared with your social media friends.

3. Do not use social media as your primary method for social interaction. Social media can make some people feel supported and important but for many, it has an isolating effect.

4. Do not use social media as a sole way to form opinions about people's holistic state. Remember that social media is only a small representation of your friends/families' lives. Social media feeds on vanity – it is an environment where most people share and tailor content that presents them at their best. Just because someone always presents the most positive information about themselves does not mean that they or their life is perfect.

5. Do not use social media if it consistently produces significant emotional experiences for you whether they are good or bad. This can create a normal pattern of emotional roller coasters in your life.

There are 5 ways to interact on social media that can optimize and enhance well-being. Be mindful of your online social life, just as you would be mindful about friends in the real world.

1. Use social media in a positive manner. Do not use it to get attention, be negative or dramatic.

2. Only use social media when you are engaging in other meaningful activities that are good for you such as getting outside, interacting with people in daily life, exercising, etc.

3. Reach out to nearby friends and ask them to join you for coffee.

4. Reconnect with old friends.

5. Connect with new people who have shared interests – this is best done through joining/liking targeted groups.

Kevin Greif has a healthy perspective. He says: "Spend your time focusing your energy on what's real in your life — the people who are there for you, your talents, your health, and whatever holds meaning for you. Then, these will increase, and bring you more abundance — and more self-esteem. Every mindless minute that is spent seeking approval on Facebook means less energy that can be used to build your life and manifest your dreams."

18

Ditching Old Friends

When I first met my ex-fiancé, he had an established group of friends from his high school and college days. Most of them lived over an hour away and slowly I was introduced to them and able to take some time to get to know them. A couple we remained 'friends' with until we broke up was not very friendly or accommodating to me (and my son) early on in our relationship. In this moment, I chose to welcome this couple with open arms and kindly tolerated their behavior because they were longtime friends of my ex- fiancé. I found out later that they did not take me seriously because they were not sure if my ex- fiancé was taking me seriously.

As I spent more time with this couple, I realized that many of our values and priorities were not aligned. In some areas we became closer and they began to treat me more cordially. As time has progressed, their priorities shifted but their mindset on some of my core beliefs did not. My ex-fiancé admitted that his core beliefs were also not congruent with this couple's beliefs, but he was not ready to fully abandon the friendship. I ended this friendship when I broke up with my fiancé.

What is the value of our "friendships"? Are you changing and are your friends changing at the same pace? Do your friends resent some of your changes?

We start out with certain friends, but as we mature, we may find that our friends have not changed or their core values have advanced in a manner inconsistent with our own need to change or we may just find ourselves having less friends. It is okay to leave friends that you have had for a long time if your values are no longer congruent but why do we have such a hard time doing so? As we move from one phase of our lives to another, we should do a friendship cleanse.

All changes...have their melancholy; for
what we leave behind is a part of
ourselves; we must die to one life before
we can enter another.

— Anatole France —

Ask yourself a few questions. Who are your real friends inside? Are the people you surround yourself with walking with you or in front of you? If they are behind you, how far back are they? Are they pushing you back to square one?

To keep progressing to our best self, we must recognize the transformation occurring within us. If we allow ourselves to get comfortable in old worthless friendships, then we are settling for something other than our best. You wouldn't pick someone to pace you in a race that runs slower than you.

Now, it is key to take the initiative and seek out people who encourage the best in us rather than undermine it. Do not be afraid to make new friends.

See Yourself and See Me Too

In Treasure Yourself, Miranda Kerr says that "what you see in yourself is what you see in everyone else around you". Self-image is your mental picture of yourself or your self-perception. It is the feelings and images that you feel and see when you think of yourself.

Let's think about this for a minute. When you are alone, what do you see inside?

Someone of a healthy mind sees themselves as they are (realism) with all their strengths, weaknesses, flaws, and perfections. Combine that with confidence and belief (positivity) in you and your abilities against all odds and you will have created a self-image. A healthy mind thinks realistic and positive thoughts about self.

Often, if we evaluate ourselves and others, it is purely from a materialistic perspective. We look at their credentials, their home, their finances, their physical appearance, and their performance. They may appear to have everything, but how do they treat others? This can be reflective of their self-image. There are people who may not appear to be doing well from a materialistic standpoint, but they treat others well and have a positive self-image.

Poor self-image may be the result of accumulated criticisms that the person collected as a child. Children are extremely vulnerable to accepting negative judgments from authority figures because they have yet to develop competency in evaluating such reports. Also, adolescents are highly targeted to suffer from poor body image issues. Individuals that already exhibit a low-sense of self-worth may be vulnerable to develop social disorders. (Source: Wikipedia)

This is not to say that a negative self-image is a terrible thing. Sometimes this can encourage us to grow, work harder or change in a necessary area. If you find yourself constantly experiencing poor self-image, ask yourself if you were criticized a lot as a child. Ask yourself if you are a bit of a perfectionist or a person with a Type A personality. Examine whether you often set the standard for success above attainable levels and whether you find yourself to be constantly disappointed by failures.

As adults, we can conduct self-examination and to consciously make strides towards correcting our self-image and making it more realistic and positive. How you view yourself dramatically impacts how you feel and act towards others.

20

Awaiting the Beauty of Flying

(18 January 2001)

As I have journeyed through life, I have walked most of the way slowly and treacherously. It has been a long journey. At about age 16, I began to shelter myself inside a cocoon. The world became a dirty place to live, a place full of sin, and a tunnel of whirling temptation. My life began to turn upside down following all the wrong turns and dips. All the chosen expectations were not being achieved, and temporary happiness was gained. In search of love and happiness, my heart swayed into the darkness of the streets and ghetto homes. It compromised all the eternal happiness we see before us — a loving family, best friends, self confidence in the inner beauty that lies within.

In a cocoon I remain. I search and wait for the beauty to rise and grow. In a cocoon I remain until fully developed into the perfect image, the image that will turn heads and make smiles. The image that will last until the wind tears into it fiercely at the end of my life and then it will be diminished forever.

The white shelter keeps feelings and emotions wrapped inside warming to perfection. It shapes hatred into love, discrimination into fairness, and despair into hope. It turns my eyes into a place of rest for other souls and glimmering balls into which all will stare. So, you ask, what is it that symbolizes me and my life?

It is a butterfly, a beautiful colorful butterfly that flies through the blue skies with no worries. The butterfly that exposes itself in its fullest beauty and grace. My wings are almost dry, waiting to feel the fresh clean air and see the shining sky reflect beauty. A walking caterpillar lived in a cocoon and came out as a beautiful butterfly.

21

Being A Lifelong Learner

As you go through the day, do you think about your purpose?

I do...I have long wondered what my purpose in life is. Some people (at these who believe in the pursuit of purpose) say it can take a pivotal moment to realize our true purpose. Maybe it is simpler than that...overthinking is not always a good thing. One morning I realized that one thing is for sure. There is something we can learn from every person we encounter. The key is finding something small each day to learn and knowing that you are someone's opportunity to learn too! If you sit back, watch intently, and listen instead of always being in the "response mode", you will be surprised at what you can learn. Is the purpose of every human being to learn?

Think of the world as a school – everything you see and interact with is a teacher. In Spiritual Growth Tip 285, Dr. Joshua David Stone and Gloria Excelsias share with us the following for reflection: "The drunk in the gutter teaches you compassion and the pitfalls of alcohol. The traffic jam teaches you patience. Nature teaches you about your Divine nature. The boss yelling at you teaches you personal power, forgiveness and invulnerability. Your spouse betraying you teaches you that you do not need anyone outside of self to make you complete but that you are whole and complete within self. The car accident teaches you to keep your mind and attention focused while driving. The stressful mother-in-law teaches you that all stress is self-created and in your mind."

The point is that perhaps our purpose on a day-to-day basis is to just learn. Seize every opportunity to learn and be thankful that you can learn and adapt and improve. If we can see each day as a blessing from this perspective, then surely there are no days to regret, and every day is one to be present in and look forward to!

22

Living A Life Without Secrets

Leading up to my son's 2nd grade Back to School party, I was anxious about him making friends after he arrived at the playground and proceeded to hide in one of the tubular tunnels on the playground. As the party went on, he began to socialize a little bit and one boy he had known from the previous year approached him near the end of the party in front of me. He tried to coerce my son to come closer to him, so he could whisper something in his ear. I told the boy that it was okay for me to hear the discussion, and he said that he preferred for me not to hear it. Now amongst 8-year-old boys, there are few conversations that should be inappropriate for parents to hear. Naturally, I became concerned about this.

Later, my son said he could not hear what the boy had told him, but, one thing was certain – I was not supposed to know! I told my son that I felt he should be careful around this child and to ensure the child did not encourage him to participate in activities that would get him into trouble. Luckily, the child was not in his classroom and this would limit their exposure to one another.

This incident got me thinking about secrets. I have a LOT of 'secrets' that I have held with me throughout my life. They are mostly mine; I am the custodian of most of my secrets. Most of them are from my past. These days I rarely do anything that requires secrecy. Most of my secrets surround relationships I have had with people and there seems to be little value in sharing those now.

Some people say that revealing your secrets can unlock more love between you and your friends and your significant other. What do you think? Can revealing secrets make a connection stronger? I'm not sure that I agree. I went through a relationship with someone where I did reveal all my life's secrets, and it created more room for criticism than anything. There was little relief and more revisiting of experiences with an intent to make me feel guilty about decisions I had made and to make my future seem tainted forever based on past decision-making trends. What I do know is that through this experience of being open, I did know how that person really felt about me!

Throughout the journey of brownBerry Books, I may choose to reveal some of these secrets but let me be clear — It is MY story to tell. I tell the stories knowing that someone could harm me by gossiping about it and inferring what my future potential is based upon it. I also tell the story for the purpose of sharing the lessons I have learned.

Have you heard the phrase — You are only as sick as your secrets? When one determines that they will walk on a path of integrity, they feel the freedom to discuss their shortcomings with others. There is no shame in that! If it makes you feel more authentic and connected, then share your shortcomings. Also share your intentions for future behavioral shifts. If people judge you for them, then so be it. At least you will have started living an authentic and real life.

When you begin to live life without secrecy, you may begin to feel like you are naked and vulnerable. This is because you stop trying to protect your vulnerability and you stop hiding from embarrassment of actions that may have been shameful. This is just the first step in coming to terms with who you are and becoming comfortable presenting yourself just the way you are. You suddenly will stop wondering what people think of you. You will know because you won't be hiding anymore. Your inner and shared worlds begin to merge.

What a blessing to know what people think of the "authentic you", and to be able to choose your inner circle accordingly!

23

What If Our Memories Do Not Match?

I was watching the TV show *Iyanla: Fix My Life*, and one season opener was focused on Jay Williams, a successful video producer who fathered 34 children with 17 women. Midway through the episode, Jay's mother and father were discussing their memories of whether they engaged in an abusive relationship. There are a multitude of reasons why their memories may have varied, but one would think that if there was physical violence, the memory would commonly exist on some level with both parties. After first denying the existence of a violent relationship, Jay's father eventually admitted that he did engage in a physically abusive relationship with Jay's mother. Finally, after decades of denial by his father, Jay knew that his mother's account was truthful.

This episode rang home for me as I recalled one holiday where all my siblings and our mother were together. This rarely occurs since we all live in different states, and, on this holiday, we were discussing childhood memories. Regarding one memory, my mother had no recollection and all four children had the same recollection. At this point, I decided that if my mother did not remember things exactly as I did, it did not matter.

What you remember is not always what the other person remembers, and this difference is irrelevant to your healing. If you are waiting on the other person to have the same memory as you, you are wasting your time...they never will! Memory alteration or suppression, whether conscious or unconscious, occurs in relationships, friendships, business transactions, etc. How many times have you remembered a connection or encounter differently from the other person? It probably happens more than you realize. As a simple example, think about how witness accounts of a crime widely vary.

Our accounts of our life experiences vary! Acknowledge the memory of others – you do not have to share the memory to acknowledge its existence. I believe a place of healing is one where we respect individual memories and elevate ourselves to acknowledge that while memories differ, they can and do exist this way.

MAGNOLIA

We are all entitled to our experiences, and we may deny memories out of pride or to avoid embarrassment or to save face...but to what end? What we cannot remember may still be a reality to someone else. So, if someone remembers something differently, the most we can do is respect their memory and understand that healing can only occur within ourselves and others through acknowledgement and resolution of the memories as they exist.

How Quickly Do You Course Correct?

We know that life is not a straight road. Life is a highway with detours that require us to take curvy and sometimes unlit back roads. Sometimes we can go fast, sometimes we must slow down, sometimes we must follow someone, sometimes we must go around someone, sometimes we break down, and sometimes we must ask for help. When your life appears to get derailed, how quickly do you course correct? Do you panic or proceed with caution?

You cannot plan detours. They appear without warning and the duration is often not revealed at first. In July 2012, my cousin's wife Beth was diagnosed with leukemia. For many months following this diagnosis, I struggled with the question "why". With 7 young children, she was not prepared for this detour. She knew a storm was coming but she did not know it would be this! She was given a 50% change of beating leukemia.

Throughout the first two years following the diagnosis, Beth's healing came through chemotherapy, many medications, radiation, good nutrition, a hearty spirit and a massive support system. She says she has never worried about the needs of her children and husband. She relinquished control of her family when her detour left her with absolutely no energy to keep holding the wheel. Beth survived her cancer treatment and climbed out of what probably seemed like the lowest valley and undoubtedly the longest detour of her life at the time. Beth is an inspiration to me.

Some detours are rough, and, for Beth and her family, the journey of leukemia was more uncertain than any journey they had ever taken. I watched them slow down – taking one minute, one hour, one day at a time. They became observant and aware and drew upon every resource they had for love and support. The purpose of their detour is no doubt still being revealed to them. One thing I know for sure is that you are meant to be on every detour you find yourself on. You will be privileged to learn many lessons on a detour. Some of the lessons Beth shared were how she learned to lean on her husband and others to keep her going both physically and mentally, how she learned the value of words as an expression of love as encouraging letters poured in, and how she learned to stop feeling guilty for resting.

Remember that highway you travel on every day? When you must take a detour, suddenly you appreciate the old highway but then, you must commit to moving. Detours serve the purpose of keeping us moving forward. Going back is not an option. For Beth, going back meant dying. Do not despair about how difficult and unfair life is; sorry, but this is not going to change things. No amount of complaining would change Beth's diagnosis. And if she dared to turn around, she would lose sight of the vision of healing. For her, time was of the essence with every medical procedure and turning back only meant that valuable time will be wasted.

When you are on a detour, you may want to believe that you are on the journey alone. Never think that your experience is unique to you. The minute you do, you lose sight of lots of resources available to help you get through the journey. Do not isolate yourself. If you look around and keep walking, you will meet others who have been taken down the same road as you (that is if you are willing to acknowledge their story and the fact that you are walking in their footsteps on the path they have already taken). There is certainly more to people than meets the eye. I encourage you to press through the journey with acceptance of areas you cannot control and with focus on the aspects that are within your control.

See any detour as an opportunity to experience new things.

— H. Jackson Brown, Jr. —

The title of this article is "How Quickly Do You Course Correct?" The speed at which you course correct is dependent upon your attitude. Course correction is not about turning around and going back on the old road; it is about taking the detour when you come to a road block. The detour is the correction. Course correction requires us to move forward on the detour with the best attitude possible. The sooner you do this, the sooner you begin the climb out of the valley.

25

What Is Waking Up?

Waking up is your opportunity to move in the direction of your best self. Buddha once said that "every morning we are born again". What a revelation! Of course, this is not literally true, but the truth is that each day starts with your intention. How will you approach the new day?

Each morning when I open my eyes I say to myself: I, not events, have the power to make me happy or unhappy today. I can choose which it shall be. Yesterday is dead, tomorrow hasn't arrived yet. I have just one day, today, and I'm going to be happy in it.

— Groucho Marx —

Each day when you wake up, seize the opportunity to start moving in the right direction. Smile when you first open your eyes!

Next, think of five reasons to be grateful. Really count your blessings. Sometimes I use the drive to work or the walk from my car into my work building to do this. I also typically use the walk into work to remind myself of a few key areas that I would like to work on that day regarding moving in the direction of my best self. Sometimes I have the same area for a long time...becoming our best self is hard work.

Finally, allow yourself to be confident and positive about the day ahead. Give yourself permission to begin the day with joy. When you encounter people in the morning, communicate joy to them. Acknowledge their presence!

As you go through the day, remind yourself that it is okay to focus on what is right. Do not we naturally focus on what is wrong? Choosing to be joyful by choosing our attitude in each moment means that we prioritize joy and happiness above all. Choose a positive affirmation to repeat to yourself when the going gets tough. One of my favorites is "joy is in me".

26

Living Life In Balance

In 2008, I went to Florida to see my little sister. She was a poor college student at University of Miami. Neither of us had money for me to stay in a hotel so I was to stay on the floor in her crowded dorm room. I had come for 10 days and was also supposed to perform a recruiting assistance job for the United States Air Force during my stay. On the first night of my stay, I went with an old college roommate and her father to a bar and met a man named Sergio. We had a brief discussion during which we both agreed that we would like to be married and to have children. I also informed Sergio that I was moving to Japan in two months. I figured this would be a showstopper – but as fate would have it, he said he would move there with me! Too good to be true?

My college roommate had also met a man in the bar and we decided to follow the two guys to the next bar. Her father was adamant that this was a terrible and dangerous idea, but we weren't listening. After this encounter, I didn't spend any time with my sister during that visit; I spent all my time at the apartment that Sergio had in Miami. I was smitten and five days later, I went to the Miami-Dade Courthouse and got married. Sergio's mother gave me a fake diamond ring as a gift. Sergio's family held a celebratory dinner for us. Later, we went to a flea market and bought two ten-dollar wedding bands to wear. I wore this wedding band for four years.

At this point in my life, I was tired of meeting guys who were not serious about any form of commitment. I was willing to leap to find love and I thought that two people could make any relationship work if they really wanted. I had to tell my story of a rushed marriage early and often. Several days after the marriage ceremony, I was required to take a polygraph test for a security clearance in Alabama. I then had to reveal that I had just married a foreign national without fulfilling the expected prerequisites.

At this point, I still had not informed family or friends. My friends began to put clues together when a man showed up at the military base to see me, and I got him a dependent military identification card. Finally, I confided in a friend that I had gotten married.

I am sure she thought I was crazy. I felt embarrassed, but at the same time, the fantasy and dream of married life was exhilarating.

> *Life goes on and we find some of it as palatable and agreeable or over-agreeable and some of it to be unpalatable. But all of it is for our benefit. All of it...so your ability not to use all of it, the good and the bad parts of it, is certainly a handicap for you. And in that area, I do wish you well, so that you can reach a stage to overcome that handicap.*
>
> — Michael Beloved —
>
> (excerpt from letter to me from my father written on March 9, 2002 when I was 20 years old)

I showed up for my military job in Japan eight weeks later and had to now tell my boss that I could not do the job she expected me to do because my security clearance had to be reopened due to my decision to marry a foreign national. That took an entire year to resolve. In the meantime, I had alienated myself from my family and friends by making a life altering decision without a single consultation. And now, to top things off, I was in a foreign nation far away from home. But I was living my fairy tale!

I took a shortcut to avoid all the hurt and real work of finding a successful relationship to be in. I "cut to the chase". So how did it all turn out? After four years and one son, I decided to sever the relationship as it stood for many reasons which I will not detail here out of consideration for my ex-husband.

Today, I have a reasonably amicable relationship with my son's father with regards to my parenting responsibility. I am now married to a wonderful man.

We all make those "what the hell was I thinking – oh wait, I was not thinking" decisions in life. If you have made one recently, life isn't over – you have dived into a situation with an opportunity to learn. You usually cannot reverse the decision once you have made it. I learned that no one wants to hear your excuses. Everyone wants you to be honest and take responsibility. No one is going to come clean up your mess.

The statement "you made your bed -- now lie in it" rang true! No matter what decisions you make in your life, make sure you are committed to getting through the tough times. Once you are going through that tough time, you might as well take the opportunity to learn your lessons. That is right – a tough time is an opportunity.

Life is best lived with balance. Use all of life...all of it to learn your lessons!

27

Caring Without Discrimination

According to Merriam Webster, there are three common definitions of "discrimination":

- the practice of unfairly treating a person or group of people differently from other people or groups of people

- the ability to recognize the difference between things that are of good quality and those that are not

- the ability to understand that one thing is different from another thing

*We are here to take care of ourselves
and others with no discrimination as
we go through our lives enjoying each
moment.*

— Scott Wiley —

The last two definitions are good abilities to possess but it is the practice of unfair treatment that we should focus on for our own self-improvement.

I found it interesting that when it came to "discrimination", the definition used the word "practice". Merriam Webster gives three common definitions of "practice":

- to do something again and again in order to become better at it

- to do (something) regularly or constantly as an ordinary part of your life

- to live according to the customs and teachings of (a religion)

This implies that when we are discriminating, we are regularly doing it (consciously and subconsciously) and we may be doing it based on customs or teachings we have learned or picked up along the journey of life.

Today, try to identify ways in which you are unfairly treating yourself and others. This can be in thought or in action. Just because you have always been doing it or because everyone around you does it does not mean it is the right or humane thing to do.

Everyone can do something to stop discrimination on a personal level. It starts with the identification and examination of the belief system that grounds you. Understand where your beliefs originated and whether you follow them out of habit or because they are truly fundamental to your being. Take on opportunities to challenge your beliefs by meeting new people and going to new places. Ask questions and listen to others' perspectives. Question facts, statistics, and rumors. Find the truth.

You are one piece of the puzzle and so am I – I invite you to connect with me by creating inner and outer environments where people are treated with dignity and respect.

28

Defining the Worth of People

Have you ever considered yourself to be a teacher of self- worth? Do you define other's self-worth through your actions?

When I sold my first home and bought a second home, I took the opportunity to employ a lady who said she wanted to earn some extra cash doing house cleaning through a mother's group I was a part of on Facebook. I needed both homes cleaned so they could be occupied in a hygienic state. When I completed the final walk through of the home I was buying, it was in impeccable condition and did not require cleaning. This left one home that would need to be cleaned – the home I was moving out of.

The lady I asked to clean the homes could not name her price and asked me to suggest one, so I offered her $150 to clean my home. It was a one-time service, and I was not sure how much effort it would require. On the day of the cleaning, she messaged me to tell me that she had fallen sick the night before and would need to reschedule if I could do so. I informed her that I could not reschedule because the new owner would take possession that day.

Two hours later, she came to the home to clean and, by this time, I was already there cleaning with my son. I thought the extra help could be used since she wasn't feeling well and probably couldn't clean as fast in that condition. When the cleaning was over, I toiled with whether to pay her the $150 I had promised. She had been late due to being sick and I had to help clean the home to ensure that it was completed on time.

I thought back to my childhood days and watching my father work as a janitor for over a decade at Main Street United Methodist Church in Hattiesburg, Mississippi. I thought about how much I thought he would be worth and how hard he worked behind the scenes. I remember that over all those years he was only paid minimum wage to do the job of a janitor, a job which no one who attended the church was willing to take on.

So, what does a janitor do? I urge you to read an excellent piece written by a janitor in the downtown San Francisco Financial District at https://libcom.org/library/it-takes-janitor-tell-tale.

When the home was cleaned to my satisfaction, the lady said she could not accept the $150 because she felt like she had not earned that amount of money. I asked her how much she wanted to be paid and she suggested $50. I told her that the least I was going to pay her was $100, and she would have to accept that for the three hours of work she had done. She unwillingly accepted the money. I hope she will look back on this experience with a heightened awareness of her self-worth.

There are no jobs beneath any one of us. If you would ask someone else to clean your mess, you should explore cleaning it yourself at least once and then determine how much that job is worth. Remember that we teach a lot about the worth we place on people by our actions. In this moment, I saw an opportunity to show a woman that she was worth a lot even if she spent her time cleaning my house. Cleaning my house was an important task I needed to accomplish in order to transfer the home to a new owner. She took part in closing a chapter in my life and that made her very important to me! My actions demonstrated that.

For some inspiration, read about Mr. Bill Crawford, a janitor at the Air Force Academy and read about the surprise reveal of his history at http://www.homeofheroes.com/profiles/profiles_c rawford_10lessons.html!

Why We Should Magnify Strength

I once saw a picture quote that said "compliment people – magnify their strengths not weaknesses". This quote spoke to me because at some points in my life, I found myself homing in what I perceive to be the weaknesses of people. I was like a shark attacking their weaknesses, and I am ashamed to admit this.

Let us discuss authentic complimenting, the magnification of strength, and negative feedback.

When we watch any competition show on TV such as American Idol, we often find that producers cast two opposing personalities. The most prominent pair that comes to my mind is Paula Abdul and Simon Cowell. Paula was the type on the show who would say something positive about everyone whether they were good or bad. Simon was the brutally honest type who people perceived as rude. He did not notice the good things about contestants; he frequently homed in on the areas they could improve but perhaps he was the most helpful person for the contestants to meet because his feedback was authentic and productive. When I think about whom I would want to be my friend, I would choose Simon – probably because I feel that we are alike.

I often wondered if I was not good at giving compliments. After some self-examination, I found that I choose to give compliments to some people more than other people. I find myself more critical of people closer to me like my immediate family and close friends.

People prefer receiving compliments even though this may not necessarily provide them the best feedback for self- improvement. People need to feel noticed and loved.

The key here is to practice actively looking for something to compliment and then genuinely offering praise. For me, there are certain people that I need to practice this with. I do not go through my day criticizing everyone, but there are some people I have found I am naturally more apt to be critical of. I want something positive to be the first thing that comes to mind with these people instead of something consistently negative. I can still be my natural honest and "to the point" self while improving my ability to magnify strengths of people.

I do not feel good when I am criticizing others. At the end of the conversation, I feel selfish and negative. The feeling of negativity that accompanies the act of criticizing exists because sometimes criticizing others means we have chosen to focus on ourselves instead of others. I am not advocating stopping or avoiding criticism, but there is a time and a place for it and it should not be the standard way of communicating. I have no hidden agenda for giving the negative feedback because I always hope that it will be used to improve his/her/our life, but sometimes I do not choose the right moment to share the criticisms.

It is equally important to recognize that if you are a person who does receive negative feedback from time to time (and we all do!), then you must become better at using the feedback to improve yourself instead of letting it drag you to and through emotional valleys. Do not focus on the fact that someone is criticizing you. Instead, think of how you can become stronger in an area by paying attention to the feedback. By failing to magnify peoples' strengths, we are somewhat culpable for their negative attitude towards criticism.

I intend to practice the magnification of strengths until it becomes habitual.

Consistent and authentic compliments result in improved self-esteem and well-being. When you gain the trust of others by authentically magnifying their strengths, they will feel more comfortable revealing their authentic self to you. Then the conversation naturally becomes one where both parties can focus on self-improvement. This is, after all, what we exist to do – find and share our authentic self!

30

The Edge Of The Cliff

Life often presents itself in the form of peaks and valleys. If we are climbing out of the valley, we are always trying to reach a peak and if we are at the peak, we seem to be on the verge of going off the cliff or there is another peak in sight that we are under pressure to climb. Have you ever felt like you are at the edge of the cliff and people are trying to push you over the edge or you have walked too close to the edge and cannot pull yourself back? That can be a very scary and uncertain time. A family member I know is currently experiencing a relationship breakup and career problems and this had the potential to threaten the life he had imagined and dreamed of.

Use what you've been through as fuel,
believe in yourself and be unstoppable!

— Yvonne Pierre —

The truth of the matter is that I still believe that this individual is and can continue to be a success in life. I know he is not alone in this experience and I can remember many periods of uncertainty in my own personal and professional life. The key is what you do during this period. As a friend, I encouraged him to keep pressing forward. Here are some thoughts I have for you if you are in a similar place.

1. <u>Do the job you are doing and do it well</u>. Never put your head down. Opportunities are always around the corner and if your head isn't up, you will miss them. When you put your head down, others perceive your negative response to failure as a mirror of what your future performance will be and you will not be first person they think of for new opportunities. Be eternally visionary.

2. <u>Surround yourself with people who believe in you</u>. When you are struggling to believe in yourself, call on these people for encouragement and use their advice to propel you to take small steps forward. Fight the negative self-talk and begin to believe in yourself.

3. <u>Focus on self-improvement</u>. I often get the impression that people regard self-improvement as a worthless endeavor...that there is no real gain from all the reading and thinking about self-

improvement. Thoughts can and often do materialize into action. We all must start somewhere and find the motivators that drive us towards the lifelong endeavor to improve.

Every adversity, every failure and every heartache carries with it the seed of an equivalent or a greater benefit.

— Napoleon Hill —

4. <u>Have an attitude of gratitude</u>. In the positions most of us find ourselves in, there are still plenty of things for which we can be grateful. I love the words of Fyodor Dostoevsky where he says that "Man is fond of counting his troubles but he does not count his joys. If he counted them up, as he ought to, he would see that every lot has enough happiness provided for it." Use this positive attitude to launch you into positive action.

31

Intentions and Perceptions

We have all had experiences where our actions have been misinterpreted by others. If our intentions were honest, there is little value in defending ourselves because this still leaves the other person feeling dissatisfied. We all want to believe that what is inside is the only real thing. I am reminded of the old saying that "perception is reality". The trouble is that both the intention and the perception are real.

We see the outside, not the inside of people. The most relevant part of ourselves often remains a mystery to those who encounter us. If we are not self-aware, we may even be a mystery to our self.

Even when we share ourselves, we may only share one small piece at a time. Rarely do we share our full selves. Therefore, most of us do our best to maneuver through life keeping the balance between intentions and perceptions because of the pitfalls of skewed or partial perceptions.

32

False Stories

How do we make sense of our hurt? Most people try to reason and make sense of why they are hurt. In the process, they create false stories about the intentions of others. The truth is that we can only understand from a level of perception which is unique to us and inherently false as a result.

The basis of your understanding of one's hurt is often a falsehood. Consequently, you may spread that falsehood causing further damage - this approach does not assist you in the process of moving on. The truth is that you feel hurt. We must guard against making the truth be the story that we create from our perspective to make sense of the hurt we feel.

You cannot transfer the hurt to others by fabricating and perpetuating a story. Trying to hurt someone will not fix the hurt you have within either. Learn to resolve hurt within yourself - be sustainable and recoverable. Shift your focus from "why am I hurting" to "what good still remains". Start with the

MAGNOLIA

smallest things...the easiest things...the sunshine, the smiles of others, the kindness of a stranger, etc.

33

Be Bob

In one episode of the show Extreme Weight Loss, Bob, a former football player and current police officer had not weighed 220 pounds since he was 14 but he was up for the challenge. He lost 228 pounds in nine months and proved that the nearly impossible was indeed possible even when enduring a knee surgery during those nine months. Mental and physical grit got him there.

As I rang in 2017, this testimony reminded me of all the people who have told me that I put too much on my plate, that my goals are too aggressive, and that my goals should be more conservative. I have been guilty of telling others these things too.

Fear drives us to doubt our abilities, set small goals, engage in comparative thinking, stumble on mental blocks and lose focus when truly transformational opportunities present themselves. Weight gain is an adversity for many, financial debt is an adversity, being in an abusive or unfulfilling relationship is a adversity....we face so many adversities.

My wish for you...and for myself...is that we will swallow our pride and tackle some areas of adversity in our lives with an unprecedented fervor.

The word fervor means an intense and passionate feeling...it is possessing passion, intensity, earnestness, enthusiasm, excitement, energy, zest, or FIRE in our approach to accomplishing the impossible. If you want something badly enough, there are NO excuses. If you fear it or do not really want to work hard for it, there are countless excuses waiting for their day of fame. So, when our "Chris Powell" shows up to motivate us, let us not retreat from the challenge. Instead, let us hold ourselves accountable and thank them for their willingness to be there by our side as we tackle our adversities. This year, I am determined to be a better writer, to share more, to be a better partner, friend, mentor, example, and mother. I am committed to healthy eating and fitness. I commit to loving myself more and to tackling the self-destructive habits I engage in. Join me in living in the present and making each day this one where we believe in ourselves and one another a lot more.

34

You Cannot Time Blessings

Ms. Nora has been busy moving around tonight...which has me thinking of getting back into the gym, but I just have not had the energy to get back into it. I have not had the morning sickness with this pregnancy, but the extreme fatigue has been kicking my butt. I have never been so tired in my life and sometimes I wish for the energy but know that my body needs the rest. I do the best that I can with what I have.

Feeling exhausted reminds me of when my ex said I needed to be in better shape to be pregnant. It is probably a good idea to be in good shape when you do conceive, but I am not in horrible shape and I felt so defeated in that moment - body image is a major issue for most women I know. It was a low life moment for me but it made me grateful for the man I have now who has never doubted the timing of our blessing.

At my healthy weight, this is not about whether I can bounce back into model shape so a man can look at me with lust and desire after childbirth. It is about trying to eat healthy and keeping my mind in a positive state despite the mental and physical fatigue I must combat daily.

It is about the miracle of life and the opportunity to impact and shape a new life in a way that I hope will be a positive and net gain for the world. Nora Wills entered the world on April 20, 1017, and I marvel each day at the blessing that she is!

Gratitude vs. Expectations

Does your paved road lead you to places of fear, stress and worry or to happiness? When we decide to practice gratitude in place of expectations, we can focus on the present instead of a place that does not exist. Let go of suffering immediately by stepping back and recognizing what is going on.

Obsession with yourself causes suffering (frustration, guilt, fear, stress) because in this state you think you will be insufficient due to something that occurs. Life is too short to feel sorry for yourself, to be angry, to be sad, to be guilty, to blame yourself or to blame others.

You cannot make real change or progress in those states. Being grateful is a survival framework for the toughest of times. Consistently find something to appreciate. Trade expectations for appreciations. Always come back to the moment of gratitude before you make important decisions so that you can be calm and collected.

Navigate from places of ease. Care less and love more. Caring is fear based.

Do not be afraid to UPGRADE the decisions that set who you are and who you are not. Spontaneously try experiences out of ordinary to create amazing and unexpected moments. Then decide to let these moments drive meaning into your soul.

36

Distractions from Self

Because it is easy, most people live lives in consistent and complete distraction...distraction from themselves because to think about who you are is hard and uncomfortable. They cannot let go of people, possessions or experiences because then they would feel alone and must face themselves.

If you keep doing what you have always done, you will keep getting what you have always gotten. Isolate yourself and discover your truth. For me, I enjoy the isolation because I like myself but, now, I struggle to connect to people, possessions and experiences. Is this worse than not knowing my truth? What am I protecting my heart from?

Perhaps I feel that if you are not vulnerable with yourself, then you do not deserve to be vulnerable with me.

Who Is Going to Love You First?

Being everything for someone or multiple people can sometimes feel like being nothing for yourself. Do you know someone who is empty and abuses the closely related concepts that "love is selfless" and "love is not selfish"? They stretch it to mean that others should have to make up for all the areas they have failed to do the work in. You may notice that this person is always unhappy no matter what you do. Such people seem hollow, unfulfilled and always wanting more. Is it you?

Be vulnerable with yourself. When you are alone sometime, ask yourself - who am I? What makes me happy? What about myself am I unhappy about? Answer the questions relative to you - not anyone else. Then establish an action you can take to address your area of unhappiness. You may need to write several actions for more than one area.

For example:

- I am a beautiful, confident, intelligent, and determined woman. I am happy when I take walks. I am not happy when I don't take a little time for myself. I will schedule time outs for myself for at least one hour per week.

Put yourself in the driver's seat. You could have said:

- I am a wonderful wife and mother. I am happy when I spend time with my husband. I am not happy when my coworker tries to boss me around. I will find a new job.

But that is too relative. Take control back and do the work. No one can replace the lack of self-love.

38

Do Not Miss

Sometimes I feel like running away from everything good. Some days my vision does not extend past my singular thought. The responsibility is too big - too grand for my comprehension most days. My to-do lists keep getting rewritten. I keep coming to the edge of missing deadlines. The bills stack up and the spending bleeds. I hide.

Everything is on the edge of falling over. It is a real game of Jenga where you try to pull something out to see what happens to me. You ask me to prioritize things differently because it will make you feel better about my choices. You make yourself feel better.

My existence motivates some and disgusts others. I choke on my history and admire it too. My confidence rises and I push my insecurities down to my feet. In painful moments, I crush them. I stand tall amid doubters because you have no idea where the veil is or how thick it is. I am in your blind spot. You see my reflection.

I do not lie but I do not tell. The judgment comes from those closest when trouble walks through the door. The thought of my offspring suffering bothers me most. But it bothers others in a way that makes them question my best. I own my best but it is a derivative of everyone I have encountered passively or actively.

My best is not your best but you mind my business so you judge me.

Why don't you just take my hand, join me in honesty about your struggles, your vulnerabilities, and your TRUTH?

Amid all of this, your confidence can still rise to the top and we can walk instead of run. We cannot race to the finish because that point is unknown. We can walk steadily moment by moment in the open knowing that even if judgment points in our direction, our best moment is now.

No, my best moment is now and you must mind your own business lest you run and miss your own best moment.

Authenticity Over Perfection

In the book Lean In: Women, Work, and The Will To Lead, Sheryl Sandberg discusses seeking and speaking our truth. She expresses hope that someday the expression of authentic emotion can in fact identify natural leaders. Recently, I took a break from writing because I was afraid to write about the experiences I had been having. Even in the workplace I was afraid to discuss them. Coworkers and friends saw me teared up for many days over the past two months and inquired why. There were times where I either broke down or came close to doing so when I normally would not have.

At this point, what I am willing to say is that someone close to me passed away and someone close to me desired to die. In the two months that I experienced these two very serious things, I also gained a promotion at work, watched a good friend get married, another friend had a baby, a niece was on the verge of arrival, I continued the best relationship of my life, and enjoyed a 10-day vacation (just to name a few positive experiences).

We often hear others say that life is about balance and while I believe that to be true, sometimes experiences remove that balance for a period. Are we more vulnerable to judgment when we are off balance? Absolutely.

What most people are not willing to admit is that the line between our personal and professional lives is often blurred. We are encouraged to keep them separate and to not be vulnerable at work. I was encouraged when I read about choosing authenticity over perfection and showing up with your whole self. To build meaningful relationships with other human beings, we should share the meaningful parts of ourselves. We must be empathetic, honest, and vulnerable.

Barbara Kingsolver says that "the very least you can do in your life is to figure out what to hope for. And the most you can do is live inside that hope".

I hope that I can continue to exist in places of vulnerability without judgment. I hope that the whole me can show up most of the time and be accepted. I hope that I can share the most meaningful parts of myself with benefit to myself and others. I hope that my authentic communication and my truth makes me the natural leader I long to be and that all my efforts serve to positively benefit others.

40

Crushing The Human Spirit

The society we live in is largely unforgiving. It is a society that wants people to live in their past of wrongs forever...to continuously suffer until the day they die. But the truth is that most wrongs and mistakes are not even known or admitted. And none of us deserve to suffer for a lifetime as a result of our wrongs.

We all deserve a chance at our redemption so that anyone who should make a mistake has hope of still creating a better version of themselves.

We never ask ourselves - what did that person experience that contributed to that mistake? That never matters...all that seems to matter is that they made the mistake. The story of Shaka Senghor highlights what is within the realm of the possible for most people who have made a mistake.

I myself am unwilling to admit all the mistakes I have made. So, who am I to judge others whose mistakes are in the open?

Shaka describes solitary confinement as an experience that will literally crush the human spirit. Think about the ways you crush the human spirit. What drives this behavior? Is it laziness, selfishness, greed, fear, or the need for control?

Should we be more willing as a society to give others a clean slate or a second chance? If you believe in forgiveness or you believe in God being the ultimate judge, then why do you support the practice of peoples' mistakes being penned into their lives for an eternity so that a mistake made in a period of seconds crushes their spirit for years, even decades repeatedly? Does it have to get PERSONAL for us to care about changing this status quo? Or is it easier to just look for a way out to say that people who make mistakes do not deserve the same chances we are afforded?

Read about Shaka Senghor's life - read his testimony - open your eyes - challenge your perspective.

Ditch The Shallow Filters

While watching Nightline, I watched a segment on the website about www.wherewhitepeoplemeet.com. It got me thinking of how I met my ex-fiancé. It was on the dating website Plenty of Fish. On this site, you can filter matches based on religion, body type, race, age, sexual orientation and other factors.

Many people turn to online dating to find love nowadays. It may not be your style, but it does work for many people. After four years of dating, I realize now that perhaps it was that initial filtering that made us incompatible - those things I had established filters with were not actually important to me, but they remained emphasis items throughout that relationship. Even when the initial signs of incompatibility were present, I still went back for more - more control, negativity, depression, judgment, etc.

Without any connection to these men on the dating website, I decided to initiate online contact to find love purely based on a filter and photos. Now I know that for me, establishing a connection and then pursuing love based on that connection is best.

With some mistakes made, some self-compassion administered, a long transition and some lessons learned, I moved forward with my life. A break up does not have to set you back - it can launch you forward. I learned that from previous relationships.

Today, I am with someone who makes me very happy and I did not use a filter to find him. I knew him for several years prior to dating him and had a connection outside of romanticism. He would have never been included in the filter I had established before...not one of the 100s of men that I searched through online to find "true love". After years of dating, we have a high degree of compatibility for many reasons that cannot simply be detected by a filter. For that, I am joyful and grateful.

42

Trust Life's Timing

Replace the fear of the unknown with curiosity which is the beginning of discovering and knowing the truth. Have an appetite for seeking and wondering.

My curiosity throughout my life has taught me so many lessons and brought me so much joy. Do not lose your inner kid spirit.

As you live each day, look for signs, paths, off ramps, shortcuts, scenic routes, and newly paved roads. You do not have to restrict yourself to the straight and narrow path. Trust the timing of unlikely events. Do not be afraid to go off the normal highway; you never know what you might find. Do the work all along to prepare yourself for the good and bad that could happen and take acceptable risks.

A Childhood Inspiration

For Working Hard: Oseola McCarty

Much of my inspiration to write and share with others can be traced back to my rural Mississippi roots. Hearing the story of Oseola McCarthy in the 9th grade was memorable. I hope it will inspire you as much as it inspired me to work hard. The article below is from The Philanthropy Hall of Fame.

Oseola McCarty was born into the world in 1908, and it was a raw start. She was conceived when her mother was raped on a wooded path in rural Mississippi as she returned from tending a sick relative. Oseola was raised in Hattiesburg by her grandmother and aunt, who cleaned houses, cooked, and took in laundry.

As a child, Oseola would come home from elementary school and iron clothes, stashing the money she earned in her doll buggy. The three women relied completely on each other, and when the aunt returned from a hospitalization unable to walk, Oseola dropped out of sixth grade to care for her, and take up her work as a washerwoman. She never returned to school.

"Work became the great good of her life," explained one person who knew her. "She found beauty in its movement and pride in its provisions. She was happy to have it and gave herself over to it with abandon."

McCarty herself put it this way: "I knew there were people who didn't have to work as hard as I did, but it didn't make me feel sad. I loved to work, and when you love to do anything, those things don't bother you. . . . Sometimes I worked straight through two or three days. I had goals I was working toward. That motivated me and I was able to push hard. . . . Work is a blessing. As long as I am living I want to be working at something. Just because I am old doesn't mean I can't work."

And hers was not a standard-issue job. McCarty scrubbed her laundry by hand on a rub board. She did try an automatic washer and dryer in the 1960s, but found that "the washing machine didn't rinse enough, and the dryer turned the whites yellow." After years of boiling clothes and then doing four fresh-water rinses, that wasn't good enough to meet her high standards. The machine was almost immediately retired, and she went back to her Maid Rite scrub board, water drawn from a nearby fire hydrant, and 100 feet of open-air clothesline.

Asked to describe her typical day, McCarty answered:

"I would go outside and start a fire under my wash pot. Then I would soak, wash, and boil a bundle of clothes. Then I would rub 'em, wrench 'em, rub 'em again, starch 'em, and hang 'em on the line. After I had all the clean clothes on the line, I would start on the next batch. I'd wash all day, and in the evenin' I'd iron until 11:00. I loved the work. The bright fire. Wrenching the wet, clean cloth. White shirts shinin' on the line."

This extraordinary work ethic, pursued straight through to her retirement at age 86, apparently produced results her customers appreciated. In 1996, Hattiesburg businessman Paul Laughlin wrote that "I know one person who still has several shirts that were last cleaned almost two years ago by Miss McCarty. He says that he does not intend to wear them; he just takes them out periodically to look at them and to enjoy the crisp fabric and its scent." McCarty, concludes Laughlin, was a walking object lesson "that all work can be performed with dignity and infused with quality."

"Hard work gives your life meaning," stated McCarty. "Everyone needs to work hard at somethin' to feel good about themselves. Every job can be done well and every day has its satisfactions. . . . If you want to feel proud of yourself, you've got to do things you can be proud of."

Shortly after she retired, McCarty did something that made many Americans very proud of her. She had begun to save almost as soon as she started working at age eight. As the money pooled up in her doll buggy, the very young girl acted. "I went to the bank and deposited. Didn't know how to do it. Went there myself. Didn't tell mama and them I was goin'."

"I commenced to save money. I never would take any of it out. I just put it in. . . . It's not the ones that make the big money, but the ones who know how to save who get ahead. You got to leave it alone long enough for it to increase."

Of course, that requires self-control and modest appetites. "My secret was contentment. I was happy with what I had," said McCarty.

These sturdy habits ran together to produce McCarty's final secret. When she retired in 1995, her hands painfully swollen with arthritis, this washerwoman who had been paid in little piles of coins and dollar bills her entire life had $280,000 in the bank.

Even more startling: she decided to give most of it away—not as a bequest, but immediately.

Setting aside just enough to live on, McCarty donated $150,000 to the University of Southern Mississippi to fund scholarships for worthy but needy students seeking the education she never had. When they found out what she had done, over 600 men and women in Hattiesburg and beyond made donations that more than tripled her original endowment. Today, the university presents several full-tuition McCarty scholarships every year.

"I can't do everything. But I can do something to help somebody. And what I can do I will do."

Like a lot of philanthropists, McCarty wanted the satisfactions of giving while living. And she succeeded. The first beneficiary of her gift, a Hattiesburg girl named Stephanie Bullock, was president of her senior class and had supportive parents, but also a twin brother, and not enough family income to send them both to college. With her McCarty Scholarship, Bullock enrolled at Southern Miss, and promptly adopted McCarty as a surrogate grandmother.

Like a lot of philanthropists, McCarty felt a powerful impulsion to act in her home region. When asked why she picked Southern Miss, she replied "because it's here." The campus (though she had never visited) was located just a couple blocks from her home.

Prior to making her gift, Oseola's one long trip had been to Niagara Falls. Here is her recollection:

"Law, the sound of the water was like the sound of the world comin' to an end. In the evening we spread blankets on the ground and ate picnic dinners. I met people from all over the world. On the return trip, we stopped in Chicago. I liked it, but was ready to get back home. I missed the place where I belonged—where I was needed and makin' a contribution. No place compares to the piece of earth where you have put down your roots."

Like a lot of faithful philanthropists, Oseola McCarty was forgiving. Reminded that the university she was giving her money to had been white-only until the 1960s, she answered with equanimity: "They used to not let colored people go out there. But now they do. And I think they should have it."

Like a lot of philanthropists, Oseola McCarty had a strong and virtuous character and good habits. She lived frugally, walking almost everywhere, including more than a mile to get her groceries. When she stayed in a hotel for the first time after coming to public attention, she made the bed before checking out.

In addition to the dignity of work, McCarty's satisfactions were the timeless ones: faith in God, family closeness, and love of locale. One friend described McCarty's faith as "as simple as the

Sermon on the Mount, and as difficult to practice." She was baptized at age 13, dunked in a local pond while dressed all in white (a mixed blessing for someone who washed her clothes by hand).

"I start each day on my knees, saying the Lord's Prayer. Then I get busy about my work," McCarty told one interviewer. "You have to accept God the best way you know how and then He'll show Himself to you. And the more you serve Him, the more able you are to serve Him."

"Some people make a lot of noise about what's wrong with the world, and they are usually blamin' somebody else. I think people who don't like the way things are need to look at themselves first. They need to get right with God and change their own ways. . . . If everybody did that, we'd be all right."

Like a lot of philanthropists, Oseola McCarty knew that giving is its own pleasure. When a journalist from People magazine asked her why she didn't spend the money she'd saved on herself, she answered with a smile that thanks to the pleasure that comes from making a gift, "I am spending it on myself."

"I am proud that I worked hard and that my money will help young people who worked hard to deserve it. I'm proud that I am leaving something positive in this world. My only regret is that I didn't have more to give."

Like a lot of philanthropists, McCarty hoped to inspire others to similar acts. And she did. In addition to the local outpouring that more than tripled her endowment, cable TV mogul Ted Turner decided to donate a billion dollars to charity after hearing her story. He was quoted in the New York Times saying, "If that little woman can give away everything she has, then I can give a billion."

And like a lot of philanthropists, Oseola McCarty knew she didn't have to save the whole world. She cast her buckets down and fixed what was at hand. "I can't do everything. But I can do something to help somebody. And what I can do I will do."

Going To Another Level

Recently at a lunch to celebrate Black History Month, a choir sang a simple but powerful song by Israel Houghton "Going to Another Level".

The lyrics are minimalist: "I'm going to another level. Don't stop reaching. Keep believing. Come on. We're going to another level. Don't stop pressing for your blessing. Come on. We're going to another level. Gotta keep pressing on."

It got me thinking...what if this was my response to life? What if I encouraged everyone, those for me and those against me, to take it to the next level?

The next level is subjective for everyone, but the point is that we can encourage one another to make progress towards positivity. This might require some work on our part. We may have to work hard to get to the next level. But sometimes, a little encouragement is exactly the boost we need. Sometimes a little constructive criticism is the boost we need.

It is about using WHATEVER you are given to advance yourself for the better. This is not a selfish act but rather a selfless act. No one may ever recognize your improvements but you have to keep pressing on, keep believing in yourself, and keep reaching. Say it and mean it - I am going to another level.

45

Who Is Your Pufferfish?

The pufferfish is the second most poisonous vertebrate in the world. Some organs of the fish, such as the liver, are extremely toxic, and can be deadly. The poison in the fish, known as tetrodotoxin, can cause numbness, high blood pressure, and muscle paralysis, which is what leads to death as the diaphragm muscles become paralyzed, disabling breathing.

Pufferfish cannot be found in the United States but many in Korea as well as Japan find some parts of the fish to be delicacies (as fugu).

Why am I writing about pufferfish?

Some people in our lives are pufferfish. No matter how we treat them, they will be toxic to us. They will numb us, paralyze us, and can even kill us. We simply lack the patience for processing them or cannot learn the proper technique.

Do not be afraid to let these people go. You may have caught them by accident but rest assured, there is someone in the world who will be happy to consume them - they will even consider that person to be a "delicacy", the "one", the "best". You do not have to keep struggling.

We do not all have the time to specially process the pufferfish. Let someone else exhaust themselves through the careful processing of the pufferfish. Let someone else present them as the perfect delicacy.

No needs to point out how close to toxicity those are who deal with the pufferfish daily. Everyone knows it. Even in its beautiful state, the puffer fish is in the shape of a Chrysanthemum, otherwise known in Japanese culture as the symbol of death.

PART 3

Short Musings

1

Stop Hiding

My health is both within my control and in control. I can maintain this through intentional acts. I can achieve fitness beyond any previous state. I will not limit myself. I will not make excuses. I will make better choices. I will prioritize myself for this is no one's responsibility but mine alone. I will not hide behind peer pressure, comfort, self-doubt, laziness, being busy, getting older, and other unspoken fears and barriers.

2

What Is Best For Me

What is best for me is already on its way to me. I move in confidence into my destiny through the peaks and valleys. Whenever life has shown me challenges, it has also presented opportunity. When life has shown me opportunity, it has shown me the needs of others. I claim and share my abundant blessings.

3

Looking Past Distractions

Looking past things and people is a learned skill. You see, everything is not meant for your dissection, processing and analysis. Learn to let certain things pass by you without your paying attention or getting sucked in. Save your energy for things that matter, not distractions. If it is meant for your attention, it will approach you with kindness. It will not jolt your spirit and surround you like a tornado. Obviously, there are outliers to this scenario but if someone or something is making you feel this way consistently, it is time to stand up, look past them/it and walk away. Do that bravely and without regret for you deserve it.

4

Prayer for Worry

Lord, bring peace to the hearts of the worried. Show them a path, hold their hand, surround them, and love them when they doubt themselves or feel hopeless. It is strength we all desire in our moments of weakness. Aid us in our times of struggle.

5

One Step At A Time

Life is so tough sometimes. The unimaginable happens but we must be resilient and relentless in our search for positivity and opportunity even when it feels like we have hit a setback. I believe in you and know that you can reach higher and achieve more than you can imagine or see. Just keep waking up each day, thanking God for that day and putting one foot in front of the other and one step at a time you will find yourself somewhere great.

6

Be A Positive Visionary

I feel overwhelmed, overloaded, and maybe even exhausted mentally and physically but despite this fatigue which is enveloping me, I have a lot to be thankful for. So, I just take a moment to think about that as I try to hold myself upright. In our struggles, we must pause for a moment to reflect and find something for which to be grateful for there is always something. Be still and it will come to you. Struggles are relative. We can always find someone struggling more or less than us. For each of us, we must assess where we are right now, avoid comparative thinking and avoid becoming enslaved to our circumstances. We must be resilient and determined...we must be positive visionaries. I seek to encourage you.

7

Turning In Your Victim Card

In the movie The Accountant, Christian Wolff's father says to him, "Life is a series of choices, none of which are new. The oldest is choosing to be a victim. Or choosing not to." We do not have to play the victim card for how we respond to life's stressors all the time. Once we realize that our response was learned, we can recognize the triggers and deliberately mitigate the impact of the event and control our response. It is intelligent, positive and productive management of self. My boss at work has a habit of always saying "it is going to be great" after discussing what might be an unenjoyable task and most of us laugh when he says it, but it completely changes how we approach a known stressful situation. We go in ready to endure, ready to accomplish, ready to learn...and we do not dwell in our misery. I am not a victim of life and I accept the challenges in front of me with joy and resilience because I know they will divinely position me where I am meant to be.

8

Past Relationships

I feel that I have been vitally part of many men's growth path but not destined to share the benefits of subsequent soul prosperity. I have been a sacrificial woman who has generated growth for the benefit of other women. The hidden truths associated with growth defy imagination and have no place but to destroy those who have learned and progressed forward.

9

Deliberate Placements

The color of your skin or your religion can exclude you from so much. Diversity is a natural part of some people's circles but not most. Diversity presents itself in many forms such as religion, race, gender, background, disability, income level etc. Consider that maybe what we should have in common is nothing because in that environment we can learn everything. The greater the discomfort, the greater the opportunity to grow.

In the unfamiliar diverse environment, I urge you to drop your defenses and simply listen with an intent to understand, not necessarily agree or disagree. Expose yourself to the experience and then allow yourself time to process what you have learned.

10

Strong Mother

Being a mother can instill a confidence, an armor, a pride, and a resilience no human can diminish.

11

Soul Destruction

Endless efforts to satisfy another's ego has destroyed many souls. Enable people to find and fill themselves.

12

Letting Go of Insignificant Things

The universe is so much bigger than me. I humble myself before that realization. The more inward I look, the less my outward situation matters and the shorter I dwell on thoughts of insignificance. I am part of something much bigger than myself or you. If I have ever been upset about something, it doesn't boil up inside of me or lie dormant...for I have it let go. Today. Moving Forward. Winning introvert life.

13

What Do You Radiate?

Conflict and fear do not reside within me. You radiate that which is within you...not that which is within others.

14

2016 Election Sentiment

It is not time to hide. It is time to survive and thrive with your head held high the entire time. Through chaos, uncertainty, fear, and disappointment lies opportunities that can benefit all people. Let us not bury our heads. Do not abandon your ship because you can't see the horizon. Be a visionary and become the master of your fate, become a more skillful sailor, and even pick up a few people lost at sea and teach them how to sail. Then one day the horizon will be in plain sight again. Let us all rise and be our best. And remember, when in doubt, be the change you want to see in the world.

15

Fresh Eyes

When you see a beautiful sunrise in the morning you do not think to yourself, "Why wasn't the sunrise so beautiful yesterday morning and the morning before?" Similarly with life, when you are having a good day just enjoy that good day. Avoid looking back at the past with sadness, judgment, regret, and disappointment. Nature recreates itself repeatedly and allows us to look with a fresh set of eyes and admire its beauty. What a simple yet powerful lesson that we can apply to humanity.

16

Spirit Survival

With the seasons changing, I am reminded of all the major changes that I have been through in my life. The key is to still find a way to be beautiful inside and out even during tough times. This is about survival of the human spirit not narcissism. If you can learn how to transition from places of hurt to places of joy, always knowing that everything will always be okay, then you will be able to better maneuver the peaks and valleys of life.

17

Never Fear The Center Of Self

Those who are too afraid of what is at the center of self begin to look to others to discover what they want. Will you be ready for your dreams when they arrive? They will arrive. Do not let them depart prematurely because you neglected to do your work. Laziness shall not be rewarded.

18

The Right Abandonment

I abandoned the energy of constant and persistent panic, insecurity, worry, doubt, pessimism and criticism and found peace and gratitude. What is your voice over for today? Is it positive? Our greatest life work is the work within. Surround yourself with people who believe that.

19

Temporary Places

Sometimes you must go down to get somewhere...but you don't have to stay there forever.

20

Choosing Compassion

Compassion can change our experience on this earth; as humans, we are always more alike than different. Judging favorably is choosing a compassionate way of being. Through this, we can harness a collective strength that can generate miracles on Earth. Judgment is enjoyed by the ego - it is the feeling that we are right and that someone else is in the wrong which separates humanity. Being thankful is the preferred approach - then one can move towards forgiveness and abandonment of grudges. Empathize with the common humanity that links you to each person on earth and be committed to being compassionate and humble. Realize that in the state of grace, you stop judging self and others.

21

Victim To Warrior

When life is off balance, it is hard to enjoy it. Sometimes just the smallest action can reset things. Often, we refuse to awaken and act and then wonder why things have generally stayed the same or gotten worse. Tipping the balance in a positive direction requires mindfulness, self-analysis and ego dismissal. Begin your balancing act now. In this moment, be more awake, aware, and unafraid than you have ever been. Look around you and assess your surroundings with clarity. Recognize whether someone or something is part of the solution or part of the problem. Then act. Time is of the essence....victims are dismissed, warriors welcome!

22

You Too Deserve Love

There will be times when you want to hit a wall, bang your head against a brick, kneel and cry, scream even, but you don't do it because anger is an outward expression of weakness. People who must express their feelings towards you in anger have lost control. You never deserve this. Support is not infinite or limitless. Clearly something else was bothering him and in his dishonesty he mistreated me. Teams is a concept of champions of all walks of life. I loved harder than anyone I knew and it was never enough so I learned to love myself and God.

23

Let The Downs Go

It was my son's thirteenth birthday. This was a day when people just happened to say the nicest things to me about him. It gave me just what I needed to feel like I was on the right track – even after thirteen years, I couldn't be sure. Then, the day ended with someone being mean to me, really mean to me. Life is ups and downs...let the downs go.

24

The Cure For Misreading

My looks did kill and I wanted to wear a mask or get botox so I could not be misread anymore. Somewhere there was a mom who only killed with looks because to really kill was too consequential.

25

Never Ever The Yelled Ones

In the end, I would miss the love, never the hate. I would miss the attachment but not the possession. I would miss the freedom but never the jealousy. I would miss the unspoken words, never the yelled words. I would miss my baby's love for sure.

26

You Hoped

The dangerous thing about writing is that you can capture the raw fleeting moments people hope would never be shared. Somewhere there is someone else glowing and dwelling or drowning in an emotion just like mine. They wanted to know that they were not alone.

27

My Baby Cries

You will have to cry because he cannot stand the look of me or the prospect of not knowing what you need or being able to give me what I deserve. Suffering is a real bitch especially when it is at the expense of someone's ego. Love always competes with the ego and because humans are humans, ego wins sometimes. You will have to cry baby, cry.

28

Too Hard

A big bump on my head from a baby bottle, soreness from abusive pumps, dry eyes from that computer full of big problems, undone late tasks with a sleeping and snoring husband next to her, a baby in her arms trying to find his way. No matter what anyone said, she knew that she had loved harder than anyone else her family had ever known, but there would still be times where her love was doubted, beyond any reasonable doubt.

brownBerry Books

A collection of books named after some of the most beautiful flowers in the world that reflect Bhakti Mary's thoughts regarding her self-improvement as she experienced life.

The brownBerry book series focuses on current well-being and preparation for a lifetime of abundant joy through sustained social, mental, and physical fitness.

The views and opinions expressed are solely hers. She encourages you to have brownBerry thoughts or discussions where you take a situation and cultivate learning by exploring its application to your self-improvement journey. We can learn much from what is happening to us and around us.

Online Resources

Email: brownberrybooks@gmail.com

Website: brownberrybooks.com

www.ingramcontent.com/pod-product-compliance
Lightning Source LLC
Chambersburg PA
CBHW072120270326
41931CB00010B/1612